Suppose I Hadn't Listened

Barbara D'Antoni Diggs

GRACE
PUBLISHING

Scripture quotations marked NIV are taken from *The Holy Bible, New International Version*. Copyright © 1973, 1978, 1984, International Bible Society. Used by permission of Zondervan. All rights reserved.

Scripture quotations marked NLT are taken from the *Holy Bible, New Living Translation*. Copyright © 1996. Used by permission of Tyndale House Publishers, Inc., Wheaton, Illinois 60189. All rights reserved.

Scripture quotations marked AMP are taken from *The Amplified Bible, Expanded Edition, Old Testament* copyright © 1965, 1987 by The Zondervan Corporation. *The Amplified New Testament* copyright © 1958, 1967 by The Lockman Foundation. Used by permission.

Scripture quotations marked KJV are taken from the *King James Version* of the Bible.

"Here Is My Life" lyrics by Ed Seabough. ©1969 Broadman Press. All rights reserved. Used with permission. CCLI #701308.

"Christmas Miracle at the Mission" previously published in *Joy to the World* copyright © 2023 by Grace Publishing House.

"Pete Bites the Dust" previously published in *Short and Sweet Too* copyright © 2017 by Grace Publishing House.

Cover Photo by Glenn Fuqua

Suppose I Hadn't Listened

ISBN-13: 978-1-60495-105-9

Copyright © 2024 by Barbara D'Antoni Diggs. Published in the U.S.A. by Grace Publishing House. All rights reserved. No part of this book may be reproduced in any form or by any electronic or mechanical means, including information storage and retrieval systems, without permission in writing, except as provided by U.S.A. Copyright law.

Dedication

THIS BOOK IS DEDICATED to my excellent interpreters in Moldova and Russia. Because of their skill and hard work, they allowed me to share the Gospel and to know the hearts of the people.

Thank you Mashie and Eugene, Moldova 1996.

Thank you Nadia, Russia 1993.

And a special thank you to Oxana, Moldova 1998, for spending endless hours at a time translating, co-teaching, helping with chores, taking care of me when I was sick, and for your joyful, servant-spirit in every situation. What a blessing you were to me!

Nadia

Mashie and Eugene

Oxana and me

CONTENTS

DEDICATION

PREFACE

ISRAEL 1973

A "Free" Trip to Israel   12

U.S.A. 1974-1982

Just Nine Days Away!   18

Christmas Miracle at the Mission   26

A Man Named Squirrel   34

Don't Stop Singing   37

Here, Lord, Take It All…Again   40

BURKINA FASO, WEST AFRICA 1983

D'Antoni Took a Long Road to Africa   48

Life in a Grass Hut   54

Motorcycle Mama   61

The Chief's Finery   66

They All Wore White   68

They Understood   71

J Z Zak a-man Song   76

Russia 1993

A Little Kindness Goes a Long Way 78

Nadia Helped Change Lives 89

Hugs, Giggles, and Kisses 95

A Night to Remember 98

Tanya, God Loves You, Too 107

Moldova 1996

Who Is Luba? 114

Sunflowers, Backpacks, and Noodles 117

Am I Being Kidnapped? 131

Birthday Party at Masha's & Whisked Off to Prison 136

God Interpreted for Us 140

Meeting the Deaf Believers 143

Saying Goodbye 146

*Letters from Transnistria,
the Unrecognized State of Moldova* 150

Moldova 1998

Map of Moldova 156

The Second Was the First 157

Tears at the Border 165

Reunited 184

Treasures in the Garden 188

Three Hours Later and I Almost Died 198

Reuniting With the Deaf Believers 205

Russian Sign Language Alphabet 211

Poor Chicken 212

Hungary 1998

To the Potatoes! 222

Russia 2004

Unexpected Visits 236

Picnic on the Ice 250

Russian Potato Salad Recipe 260

Updates on Moldovan Friends 261

Stories Just for Fun

The Uninvited Guest 264

No Child Was Eaten 269

Pete Bites the Dust 272

Now THAT's a Nice-a Meatball 274

Bran Muffin Recipe 277

Conclusion

Suppose I Hadn't Listened 280

Acknowledgments 284

Scriptures Meaningful to Me 285

About the Author 286

Preface

I'M EXCITED TO SHARE *Suppose I Hadn't Listened* with you. It's been a work-in-progress for over 50 years!

There are dozens of stories, but I've only shared 40 of my favorites here. These true stories are based on my memories and information gleaned from my travel journals.

Most stories are stand-alones. Some may overlap. There is no strict chronology. Two stories have arrivals and departures within the story; others continue the events within the trip.

In the Moldovan stories, I write about Bendery and Tiraspol. Both are located in Transnistria, the "unrecognized state" in Moldova. In this territory, Russian is spoken, and it is governed by communists although it is not a communist state. The rest of Moldova speaks some Russian, but primarily Romanian. It is a Democratic Republic.

In Moldova and Russia, all conversations were through interpretors, except once. That story is titled "God Interpreted for Us."

For your richest reading experience, I suggest reading the stories in the order presented. Blessings to each of you as you enjoy the adventure!

~ Barbara

NOTE: I take full responsibility for any errors that occur in the details. Sometimes there weren't enough hours in the day to record everything in my journal!

Israel
1973

A "Free" Trip to Israel

1973

For a week I braved the rush hour traffic between Baltimore, Maryland and Washington, D.C. On the seventh night I was asked a question. It never occurred to me my whole life would change if I answered, "Yes."

An evangelist friend held a revival in the D.C. area. I attended that October of 1972, and sang in the choir. At the end of the week, Felix Snipes, the music evangelist said, "It certainly has been good to know you. How about going to Israel with us in January?"

"Israel?" I asked. I didn't know if I could even find Israel on the map. "Okay. Send me the information."

Pondering this invitation during the hour-long drive back to Baltimore, I began to anticipate the possibility. I was 19 years old and the privilege to walk where Jesus walked was an exciting thought. "Wow, God, Israel!" I prayed. "Is it possible to even dream about this? If you want me to go, please help me work this out. Amen."

When the information arrived in the mail, I saw that the cost was $699. *Oh, my goodness! That's expensive.* It was eight weeks' salary for me. After counting the coins in my piggy bank and arranging my budget on paper, I came up with eight dollars. *This isn't going to work.*

Next, I applied for a loan at my credit union. Mr. Brown, the same man who had processed my car loan the year before, assured me there would be no problem.

But there was. I was turned down.

Mr. Brown was exasperated. "I don't understand why you were turned down. Your account is fine," he said. Then he added, "For some reason, I think you're supposed to go on this trip. I don't know you, and I'm not a Christian, but I want to personally lend you the money, interest free. Take as long as you need to pay it back."

Truly this was God's answer to my prayer!

I sent in the money for the trip by the deadline and went to Israel in January, 1973. God did some major changes in my life while I was there.

The trip was better than I ever could have imagined. I fell in love with Israel—its sights, smells, and the haunting sounds of the beautiful Jewish music.

I enjoyed everything about Israel, but it was the Sea of Galilee that captured my heart. It seemed to know me; here was something to which I could relate: the raging sea, the angry waves, the darkness, the isolation. These were similar to emotions I was trying to mask in real life, and I could run from them no longer. I stood on the bow of a ship looking over the sea when a violent storm came up. As waves crashed over the boat and torrents of rain pelted me in the face, they mingled with my tears. I cried alone, almost as violently as the storm. I looked up into the heavens and tried to communicate to God the turmoil of my soul over job, family, and self-worth. After much anguish and struggle, I was able to surrender my pain to God and sang to Him a song I had learned in choir:

> Lord, you asked for all my life in healing hurts and ending strife,
>
> With mind to always seek the truth, with voice to always speak the truth,
>
> And live to manifest Christ's worth,
>
> I cannot wait, I cannot wait!
>
> Here is my life, I want to live it,
>
> Here is my life, I want to give it serving my fellow man, doing the will of God;
>
> Here is my life, here is my life, here is my life.

It was the earnest plea of my heart. "Here, Lord, take it all. Please use me to glorify you!"

Within moments, the raging of my soul quieted and I was bathed in God's sweet, holy peace. I believe God wanted me to know He had heard my cries, because the storm on the sea abruptly came to a halt. As the inner peace flooded me, the sun popped out in magnificent brilliance, sending a shining light across the sea. Never before or since have I seen the weather change that fast. It was a very private, glorious, and awesome experience. Three simple and profound truths were revealed to me. God heard my prayer. God loved me. God showed me He heard my prayer.

I stood looking at the splendor of the mountains around me.

The boat no longer rocked in the angry waves. It gently bobbed on the water. I knew my life would be different when I returned to the States because I was a changed person. God would help me through anything.

In February, a month after returning from the trip, my friend the music evangelist phoned. "Barb," he said, "I really need you to mail me the money for the trip."

He had never received the payment I had mailed over two months earlier. It startled me. In essence I'd been to Israel, Greece, and back for free!

But God had a surprise for both of us. The very next day my friend called again. "You won't believe this," he said. "Your check arrived in the mail today, postmarked December 1, 1972!"

"Praise the Lord!" I shouted. "Go ahead and cash it."

This entire experience started a major series of events that increased my teenage faith to fully believe in the sweet blessings that God gives to His beloved children. And over the more than 50 years since that first trip, He has walked with me through a multitude of valley and mountain-top experiences. Oh, how precious He is to me! I give thanks to Him with a grateful heart.

U.S.A.
1974-1976

Just Nine Days Away!

Baltimore, 1973

God's Guidance for Bible College

MY HEART WAS BREAKING as I stuffed my clothes into the suitcase. Israel had captured my heart and now I must leave her. I wondered if I also would leave behind the new-found joy I had discovered during my Sea-of-Galilee experience.

My fears were unmerited. Even after three days in Greece, I still felt God's tender love and care toward me. Sitting on that big 747 heading back to the States, I prayed, "God, isn't there someone on this plane I can talk to about you?" A gentle nudge inside of me prompted, *"Get up and look. There is someone."* I scouted that entire plane. I was about to give up when I spotted Betty Durham, a widow and musician who had provided the music for us during our trip. She was sitting on a single seat at the back of the plane.

"You've come to talk with me, haven't you?" she asked as I approached her. "God already told me you'd be coming."

"He did?" I felt my soul leap within me. "Betty! God told us both the same thing!"

I stood in the aisle as we talked for five hours, exchanged phone numbers, and thus, began a friendship.

Several months later Betty invited me to Atlanta to hear Corrie ten Boom speak. In her powerful testimony, Corrie shared how God delivered her from Auschwitz during the Holocaust. The intensity of Corrie's message convicted my heart, and I also desired to share God's message to others. I knew I needed some in-depth biblical training. But where? I told Betty my thoughts and she exclaimed, "Barbara! There's a Bible college right here in Atlanta! Why don't you apply?"

With fear and faith I did apply. In August, four months later, the word came. "You've been accepted. Orientation is on …." I panicked. *Oh, my goodness! That's just nine days away! There is **no way** I can do this.*

As I reread the letter, I had WRBS Christian Radio playing in the background. I heard Ed John, the announcer, dedicating a song to me. "How strange," I thought. "Ed knows I'm at church on Wednesday nights." Then he said, "This song is titled 'His Way, Mine,' and it's sung by Betty Durham." By then my ears perked up. I knew this was no coincidence. Ed and I knew each other through my volunteer work at the station. I called him at the station and asked him how he knew to dedicate that particular song by that specific artist to me. He said he wondered the same thing, but at that particular moment he had felt led by God to do so. Now, folks, that's experiencing God!

I called Betty and told her about the letter and song.

"Praise the Lord! When are you coming?" she shouted.

I hesitated. "Betty, I know this is God's will, but I don't have the money for Bible college."

With her prophetic boldness she exclaimed, "Barbara, you've trusted God so far. Don't stop now! You can live with us—free room and board. Your bedroom is waiting. See you in nine days!" And she hung up.

Stunned, I put the phone down and started laughing, crying, and dancing all around my room. I was seeing God at work. I didn't know how, but I knew in nine days I would be sitting in orientation in Atlanta, Georgia.

Betty Durham

Surprise! Surprise! For Atlanta

To my amazement, I experienced nine days of . . . miracles. Let me tell you what God did.

The hardest part about leaving was quitting my job with The

Equitable Trust Bank. Having worked there several years, I loved the people and hated to give only one week's notice. Sad that I was leaving, my boss was unusually happy to discover I was to attend a Bible college. "I've watched you over the years," he said, "And I can see that you really are a Christian. It's right for you to go. You probably don't know this, but I'm a Christian, too. Because of your faith, I know I also can take a stand for God." My eyes filled with tears. Not only did I have my boss's blessing to leave, but I had gained a brother in Christ. The miracles were already beginning.

I applied for two separate scholarships through The Maryland Baptist State Convention and was told the deadline for applying had been two months earlier. God was working, though, because both committees (unrelated to each other) were holding emergency meetings in mid-August and I *just happened* to be at their office on the day of the meetings. Within an hour, as a courtesy to me, both committees added me to their agendas. Courtesy? Not in my opinion; it was a miracle! More amazing, both of them granted me scholarships!

Another miracle came when my girlfriend picked me up before we went out to dinner. "I forgot something and need to stop by my house first," she said. "Come in with me and you can say hi to Mom."

I had no sooner opened the door than peals of "Surprise! Surprise!" rang out. There sat all of my precious co-workers from Equitable Trust! I almost died on the spot; they startled me so. Those dear people had "all the fixings" for a dinner, and in addition, they had collected an envelope full of money as a farewell gift. Through their unselfish love and generosity I once again experienced God's confirmation about leaving.

On Sunday afternoon, my pastor's wife stopped by and asked if I would go over to the church and run through a song with her. "Sure," I said. Since the church was across the street from my house, I asked, "Is it okay if I go like this?" I was barefoot, wearing cut-offs and a baggy T-shirt.

"No problem," she said. "This won't take long."

I didn't know it then, but I was about to experience another miracle. Giggling as we often did, Pauline and I opened the door to the sanctuary…and were met with a thunderous roar of "Surprise! Surprise!"

"Ahhhhhhh!" I screamed and jumped three feet into the air! It scared the liver out of me. Laughter and claps of glee filled the room. The whole church had turned out for the surprise. It worked. Crying with amazement, I opened their gifts: luggage, clothes, stamps, and money. What a blessing! After counting the money, I discovered it was exactly the amount I needed to complete my tuition fees and expenses. Praise the Lord!

God used many people to confirm His will and prepare me for my departure. In doing so, each of us had the opportunity to experience God while He worked.

Critter and Bear

Atlanta, here I come!

My father, whom I called "Bear," had crammed every nook and cranny of "Critter's" trunk and back seat with anything I could possibly need for Bible college. Yep! Critter was stuffed with all my earthly belongings.

"Critter" was my very first, "brand-new" used, 1967 Chevy,

which I had purchased a year earlier. Boy, was I proud of that car! I washed and waxed and polished her often. She gleamed like a diamond on a new bride's finger! Now she was ready to cross the state line and take me on to the next venture of my life.

"Be careful, Bear! Don't spill any coffee! Wipe your feet! Don't make a mess!"

Bear looked over at me. "We have 700 miles to go and I'm drinking coffee in here!"

Silence. I knew this was not the time for a challenge.

The journey started out well. We rolled down the windows and sang at the top of our lungs as we bounced to rock and roll on the radio. We headed up the Interstate and had driven about 40 miles when we heard a miserable sound: *thump, thump, thump, thump.* The right rear tire was not only flat, but dead. Ripped to shreds. It meant methodically unloading all of my earthly possessions right there on the highway for all the world to see.

Trucks whizzed by. I watched in horror as a few pieces of my clothes flew out the windows and onto the road. Buses zoomed too close, and the car swayed in the breeze. Digging through the valuables of my lifetime, we located the jack, only to find it wouldn't hold on the bumper.

Flashing lights appeared behind us as a state trooper had mercy on us and stopped. Not only did he have a jack that fit, he looked around at my "roadside flea market," shook his head, and decided to change the tire himself. Me? I was busy chasing "earthly belongings" and couldn't have cared less about the tire.

When Bear and I got back into the car, all I got was "the raised eyebrow." I smiled sweetly. "Nice weather, huh, Pop?" Bear decided he needed a cup of coffee to calm his nerves. I agreed, and decided a cold soft drink would taste rather good, too. We pulled off at the next exit, got our drinks and climbed back into Critter. "Be careful. Don't spill anything," I reminded Bear.

I got "the eyebrow" again.

We had no sooner pulled onto the road than I flipped over my drink. Foam and sticky liquid spewed everywhere. The seats. The dash. The back seat full of clothes, the floor and the windows.

Bear just roared and slapped his thigh. "Hah! Hah! Hah!... Ho! Ho! Ho! Serves you right for being so picky."

Critter was a mess. It humbled me and cured me at the same time. I snorted a loud hmph, then started giggling. I attempted to give Bear "the eyebrow;" instead I began to laugh. By now both of us were no good. Once again, we had to pull to the side of the road. First to calm our hysterics, then to clean up the car.

As strange as it sounds, that really did cure me. I realized I had allowed that car to become an idol to me. I had put it before God and family. God had miraculously provided all of my financial and physical needs in order for me to attend Bible College, and there I was acting spoiled and quite a bit ungrateful.

My priorities should have been to be grateful for the car, not worship it, and to make Bear comfortable on the trip. If I had done that, then I would have been free to enjoy the blessings that God already had provided.

Critter, many years after Atlanta

My father, "Bear"

Christmas Miracle at the Mission

Atlanta, 1974

"L ADIES, YOUR ATTENTION PLEASE. For a surprise, come to the dining room at 10 o'clock tonight. And wear your pajamas."

The rusty, brown intercom squawked out my strange message throughout the dingy halls of the women's rescue mission in Atlanta where, after Bible College, I lived and worked as a housemother. Flipping the intercom switch to off, I slapped my hand on my leg and chuckled. *Won't they be surprised? They'll never guess we're going to have a pajama party in the dining room.*

It was Christmas Eve, 1974. I had volunteered to work the three days of the holiday so the other staff members could go out of state to be with their families. I didn't mind, but looking around at the long, windowless hallway with ugly green walls and no decorations, I thought, "Yuck, this has got to change. And I've only got four hours to get it together."

That's when I remembered Bosco, the pink, polka-dotted hippopotamus decal on my bedroom wall. He was a cheerful-looking thing, so I decided to share him. I carefully removed the clingy decal, and then hung the huge, three-by-three foot image right outside the dining room door. Smoothing out the wrinkles, I stepped back to admire him. *Oh yeah! Definitely an improvement.* I nodded my head and grinned. *The ladies will love him.*

It wasn't long before doors squeaked open and residents on the first floor poked their heads out to gossip about the strange announcement. "Wonder why Barbara wants us to wear our pajamas to the dining room at 10 o'clock," Ethel said to Lois, who stood trying to flatten her frizzy hair into place.

"Won't we get into trouble if we're not in our rooms?" asked Marie.

Questions about the mystery evening buzzed up and down the hall. Most of the residents despised Christmas and tried to avoid it by going to bed extra early. There were too many memories they wanted to forget: drunken stupors, broken homes, fights, jail, and now life in a rescue mission…with no family.

My prayer was that curiosity would be stronger than despair. *Please God, help me to make this an extra-special Christmas for my ladies. We need you so much. Amen.*

Jean, the cook, was the only resident who knew about the surprise. After supper, she and I spent hours making batches of thick, chewy brownies with pecans. While the brownies cooked, Jean even rigged up an artificial tree she found in the basement. It looked wonderful with blinking lights, tinsel, and icicles.

At 10 P.M. instead of doing my nightly bed check, I flipped on the intercom, "Ladies, it's time to meet me in the dining room. And it's okay to wear your pj's." Padding around in my red, one-piece, footed pajamas, I was also dressed for the occasion.

More than 40 ladies lined up outside the dining room and stared at me in my makeshift Santa pajama suit.

"Surprise! Surprise!" I shouted. "We're having a pajama party. Come on in."

Each table held plates piled high with brownies, homemade Christmas cookies, and punch bowls full of hot, buttered popcorn. Jean had completed the feast by providing mugs of steaming hot cocoa. "Take all the marshmallows you want," she yelled from the kitchen. "They were donated."

Suddenly, there were cries of, "Uh, oh. Get me out of here! Help! Somebody help me. There's a pink elephant on the wall!" It was Edna. "I know'd my drinking days would catch up with me!" she yelled.

I dashed into the hallway.

"Edna, it's okay. It's a pink hippopotamus, not an elephant." I laid my hand on her arm. "I put Bosco, my hippopotamus, on the wall so it would be cheerful."

"You did?" Edna always ended her sentences with a high-pitched squeak.

"I did."

"Well, if you're sure I ain't hallucinating with DTs and he's really there, I guess it's okay. This is my first sober Christmas. I'm a little nervous," she said as she mopped her head with an old, red bandana.

"Come on, friend," I grabbed her arm. "Let's get on in to that party."

Edna gave me a toothless, lopsided grin and sniffed the air. "Mmm, sure does smell mighty good in there."

In the dining room the ladies munched on cookies, brownies,

and popcorn.

Catherine, another recovering alcoholic and our boogie-woogie piano player, sat down and rolled out a few chords. I grabbed a spoon to use as a microphone and said, "Hit it baby, give me 'Hello Dolly.' "

The ladies laughed and cheered as I belted out Louie Armstrong's rendition, rolled my eyes and shook my head as only Louie could do. Soon we were singing different show tunes, Christmas carols, and finally, "Silent Night."

It had been a tender evening. Here we were, ages 20 to 89, and we were playing like a big family of kids. Hardened hearts softened, sorrows were temporarily forgotten, and regrets put on hold. It was magical.

"Dear God," I prayed after the ladies left for bed, "Thank you so much for hearing my prayer and making this a good evening. The ladies had a blast. Amen."

Christmas morning the aroma of fresh-perked coffee and the scent of Jean's scrumptious, hot and gooey cinnamon buns floated throughout the halls of the mission.

"Oh, yum. This smells sooo good, Jean. What a difference from the usual cold cereal or oatmeal breakfast. The ladies will love this!"

Licking my lips and rubbing my stomach, I turned on the intercom and said, "Merry Christmas, ladies! Breakfast is ready."

Doors slammed as the sound of feet clomping down the steps echoed throughout the building. In less than four minutes there was a long line of hungry women standing near the dining room door.

Edna turned to a lady staring at Bosco and patted her arm.

"Don't worry, lady. You're not having DTs or nothin'. That's Bosco, a pink hippopotamus, not an elephant. Barbara said he's up there to make it cheerful for us."

I rapped on the table. "Ladies, today for a special treat, Jean and I are going to serve you breakfast in the parlor."

A voice from the back of the line spoke. "In the parlor…the off-limits parlor? Really?"

Because it was Christmas morning, I had allowed the ladies to wear pajamas and robes for breakfast. I smiled as they stood a little straighter and gracefully strolled into the parlor to find seats.

With Jean's help, around the room I had set up TV trays that held plastic carafes of steaming coffee. Arnell, the dishwasher, brought in the cinnamon rolls. I carried a pan of scrambled eggs, and Jean followed with crisp bacon. We went to each lady, poured her coffee, offered cream and sugar, and served her.

The change in the atmosphere was amazing. Finally, they accepted the title of "ladies" I insisted on calling them. For these brief hours they were no longer street women, prostitutes, drug addicts, alcoholics, and ex-cons. They were ladies dining in elegance.

After breakfast someone started singing "Rudolph the Red-Nosed Reindeer." Then came "Santa Claus Is Coming to Town," followed by "Over the River and Through the Woods." In the far corner a soft, alto voice began singing "Away in a Manger." Afterwards, another voice started "O Holy Night." Raspy, low voices sang out with fervor as they proclaimed the birth of the Christ child.

There was a hushed silence and then a voice softly spoke. "Today in the town of David a Savior has been born to you; he is Christ the Lord. Suddenly there was with the angel a multitude of heavenly hosts praising God and saying, 'Glory to God in the highest, and on earth peace and goodwill to all men.' "

It didn't matter that some of the verses were different from the Bible. We understood the meaning because we felt Christ's love present with us. It was a time of reflection and thinking about Christmases before living at the mission. There was sadness, but also a quiet joy. Today was Christmas. Things were different. There was peace.

Hating to break the spell, I whispered, "Ladies, it's time to open presents."

Cheers and shouts went up from some of the younger residents. Older ones grinned. The spell wasn't broken after all. Some scrambled for seats on the floor, while others moved to chairs closer to the tree.

A local women's auxiliary had selected and donated hundreds of beautifully-wrapped gifts for the ladies. What a sight it was! My furry, red pajamas made me an ideal Santa as I "ho, ho, ho'd" and handed out personalized gifts.

Wrapping paper scattered and colored ribbon flew as the ladies tore into their packages. Eyes became wide with excitement as treasures began to appear.

"Look at this green sweater I got," Tina, a 23-year-old prostitute said.

"New shoes! Just my size, too," toothless Annie said as she held up a shoe for inspection.

"Hey, everybody. Looky here at this nice, warm robe. My bones has been a ackin' for sumpin like this," cackled old Lula.

I clapped my hands with excitement.

Looking around, I saw Nettie wiping tears from her eyes.

Yellow wrapping paper was crumpled beside her.

"Nettie," I said, "What did you get?"

With tears streaming down her tired and weathered face, she looked up at me and said, "A used girdle and a dirty slip. And they ain't even my size. Why didn't I get sumpin new like everybody else?"

Anger welled up within me, "Oh, Nettie, I'm so sorry." I hugged her. "I don't know why this happened." I started crying, too. My 20 short years of life had not prepared me for this kind of cruelty. Our joyous celebration stopped and no one knew what to do.

Through my tears I noticed old Lula, hunched over and unsure in her steps, wading through the ribbons and bows. "Here, Nettie child, you take this here good warm robe. It'll fit ya sure 'nough."

Marie brought over the bottle of perfume she had received. She hesitated, but only slightly. Everyone knew Marie loved perfume better than anything in the world. "Here, Nettie," she said, "You take this perfume. It'll make you smell real purdy."

The idea was contagious. Hardened, bitter women—women who usually hoarded anything they got——suddenly were sharing and exchanging their gifts with one another. A miracle took place. They wanted to give. Their wealth came not from the gifts given, but from unselfish hearts full of love and compassion. Truly, we were celebrating the real spirit of Christmas.

Looking around at the ladies sitting on chairs and the floor, I wondered how they felt to be away from their families. Many had come to the mission as a last resort for shelter and care. Others were brought in by the police. Betty had told me she was "dead" to her family.

This was my first Christmas away from home, yet I was in the middle of the biggest family ever. It was strange. I was their housemother, but this Christmas these ladies became my sisters, mothers, and even my grandmothers. I dearly loved them. Young and old, black and white, addicts and prostitutes. For a short time, pain and hopelessness were forgotten. Wrinkled brows relaxed and smiles replaced frowns. The hard life of living on the street was softened by laughter, love, and unconditional acceptance. It didn't matter. We were beloved family.

A half-century later, as I think back on those days, I can still see "my ladies." I feel their pain. I sense their hopelessness. But more importantly, I remember our bond of love and the miracle that Christmas morning.

Dear Ladies,
I don't know where you are today. Most of you probably are not alive. I've never forgotten you. Thank you for allowing me to share my first Christmas away from home with you. Remember, I love you. Merry Christmas, and may God's grace and peace bless you forever.

With love,
Barbara, your Housemother

A Man Named Squirrel

Atlanta, 1974

Darkness settled around me as I sat alone in a parked car on a desolate street in downtown Atlanta. It was Saturday night, and part of my job as a housemother for the women's mission was to pick up residents after meetings. As I waited, I watched a man carrying a brown paper bag stagger all over the street. He spotted me at the same time, changed direction and headed toward my car. I would have driven away, but I knew the mission's old clunker car would never start without a lot of coaxing and kicking. Boy! Was I scared! I prayed, "Help me, God. Thank you. Amen." I immediately sensed the Lord's presence calming my fear. And it was just in time, because the man leaned into my car window.

"What's a pretty thing like you doing sitting here all alone in downtown?" he asked.

"I'm waiting for some friends," I replied, determined not to show my fear.

"What's your name?" he asked.

"Barbara, what's yours?"

"My name is Squirrel," he said and stuck out his hand for me to shake.

"Nice to meet you, Squirrel." I shook his hand and quickly let go.

Squirrel looked a bit wild with his matted hair sticking out in various places on his head. His clothes were filthy and matched in odor. I think he was trying to impress me because he pulled two bottles of whiskey from the paper sack, then rolled up his sleeves to reveal recent needle marks in his arms.

Squirrel gave me a friendly grin and patted my arm. I turned and looked him right in the eye.

"Squirrel, God loves you. If you were the only person on this earth, God still would have sent His son, Jesus, to die for you. He loves you that much."

Squirrel jumped back in amazement. His mouth flew open and he started to cry.

"God loves me? God…loves me? God loves me?" he exclaimed, amazed. "Nobody ever told me that before, lady." Through deep sobs he said, "Lady, the reason I came to your car was to rape you."

"Squirrel," I replied. "I'm a Christian and I belong to Jesus. I asked Him to protect me and He is. You can't touch me."

Still crying, Squirrel looked at me for a long time. Then he straightened up, turned to leave and stopped. He held out his hand to shake mine, this time in friendship.

By this time, my three ladies had quietly climbed into the car. I looked at them in my rear view mirror and saw them wide-eyed.

Squirrel turned quietly and reverently, and left, repeating

over and over again, "God loves me….God loves me…."

"Who was that?" Francine asked.

"That was Squirrel. He just found out that God loves him."

They nodded and smiled. As new believers, they understood the joy of being loved by God.

Dear Reader,

God loves you, too. Whatever your past, whatever bad things you've done, God loves you. If you were the only person alive on the earth, God would still send His son Jesus to die for you. He thinks you're special and longs for you to receive His forgiveness and know Him personally. It's His gift to you, because He already paid the price for your sins when He died on the cross and rose from the grave three days later.

Beloved, that's how much God loves you.

God so [greatly] loved and dearly prized the world, that He [even] gave His [one and] only begotten Son, so that whoever believes and trusts in Him [as Savior] should not perish, but have eternal life. John 3:16 AMP

Don't Stop Singing

Atlanta, 1976

PEGGY AND I WALKED down the long gravel driveway from where we'd parked my rental car near the woods. It was 11:30 P.M. Dark and creepy as shadows from distant streetlights reflected off the rescue mission walls. I had never enjoyed that walk when I worked at the mission. But that was our only parking area, so there was no other choice.

A recovered drug addict, Peggy still lived at the mission. We had continued our friendship even after I resigned.

This particular night was special. We'd attended the final meeting of a week-long Christian conference. Full of valuable knowledge about Biblical principles, we had a lot to discuss.

We had sung in the car all the way home from the conference and even giggled because it actually sounded fairly good. We were enjoying ourselves. Singing also kept our minds off the eerie darkness as we walked down the gravel road to the mission's front door. We continued singing the old Bill Gaither song, "There's Something About that Name."

The mission, close to downtown Atlanta, had once been a

large mansion. It was located on a small hill with two sets of steps leading down to the sidewalk and street. Since it was in a rough neighborhood, it was not unusual to encounter strange people. That night was no exception.

As we reached the mission, a man, about 50 yards away, was walking quickly down the other side of the street. His back was to us. When he heard us singing, he abruptly turned around and walked toward us with a determined stride. Even from that distance, we sensed an evil presence.

Peggy, who wasn't usually afraid of anyone or anything, ran off and left me!

The man stomped up the 17 steps from the sidewalk and marched directly to me, his hate-filled eyes never leaving my face. It seemed my feet were frozen to the spot.

Don't stop singing. The command was clear.

Normally, I would never sing in a stranger's face, but I knew that order had come from God, so I sang.

When the man was less than a foot away from me, the presence of evil was so strong it almost took away my breath.

"Jesus! Jesus! Jesus! There's just something about your name." I screamed my song over and over.

Every time I belted out the name of Jesus, the man's head and shoulder jerked to the right, then back to the left. Honestly, to this day, I believe angels socked him in the jaw with their fists. This happened four or five times. Suddenly, fear came into his eyes. The man shuddered, turned, and ran down the steps. He crossed the street and kept running.

Peggy stood on the porch with her mouth hanging open. Finally, she said, "What just happened?"

I was in shock myself.

"Peggy, we saw the power that's in the name of Jesus. I don't have words for this either, but God protected us from evil."

"Whoa. He sure did," she said. "I've *never* seen anything like that before."

"Me neither, Peggy. Me neither. But I do know God took care of us."

I'm reminded of verses from Psalm 91 (NLT):

> 2   *This I declare of the LORD:*
>   *He alone is my refuge, my place of safety;*
>   *he is my God, and I am trusting him,*
> 3   *For he will rescue you from every trap....*
> 5   *Do not be afraid of the terrors of the night,*
>   *nor fear the dangers of the day....*
> 9   *If you make the LORD your refuge,*
>   *if you make the Most High your shelter,*
> 10 *no evil will conquer you;*
>   *no plague will come near your dwelling.*
> 11 *For he orders his angels*
>   *to protect you wherever you go....*
> 14 *The LORD says, "I will rescue those who love me.*
>   *I will protect those who trust in my name.*
> 15 *When they call on me, I will answer;*
>   *I will be with them in trouble.*
>   *I will rescue them and honor them."*

That night we experienced exactly what these Scripture verses state.

Here, Lord, Take It All…Again

Tennessee, 1979

I'll never forget that week in April, 1979. My church, First Baptist in Morristown, Tennessee, held a World Missions Conference. I talked with God beforehand and asked, no not asked, I *told* Him not to bother me during the conference. I wanted to enjoy what the speakers had to say.

Wow! It was a glorious week hearing the stories of each missionary!

I was okay, and God obliged my demand until we sang the final hymn on Sunday morning. Then my internal conversations with God became like a noisy battlefield.

For years God had prompted me to surrender to foreign missions. My response? "No way, God. I'm *not* going! And that's that!"

Now, the question came once more. *Will you go, Barbara?*

I grabbed the back of the pew, screwed up my face and shook my head. *No. I'm not going!* Irritated with God for bringing this up again I left church in an angry huff.

God always has a plan for our lives. Whether we listen to it, or obey it, is another story. I drove home, slammed the car door and stomped into my house. I turned on my stereo to listen to a Christian station. Surely this music would soothe my angry soul.

Did it? Of course not! The first song that came on was "I Surrender All."

Hmph.

Yet I continued to listen. Maybe something pleasant would come on next. The second song started, "Wherever He Leads, I'll Go."

I looked up at the ceiling. "God, this is not making me feel better. What's up?" Turning off the stereo, I fixed lunch but couldn't eat it.

There was no peace. Anger boiled within me. "Okay, God, okay. I'll go to the motel and at least talk with the missionaries who spoke this morning."

The motel was only a mile from my house. I drove over, pulled into guest parking, got the room number from the desk clerk and marched up the steps to the second floor. After knocking on the door several times and getting no answer, I turned to go back down the steps.

That's when Ted Cox and his wife, Pat, missionaries to Japan, stepped out of their car. Ted, yelled from the parking lot, "Miss, did you want to talk with us?"

"No, sir, I didn't," I yelled back.

"But you're knocking on our door," he said.

"It wasn't my idea," I yelled back.

"Wait there, we're coming right up," he hollered back. They invited me in. He and Pat sat on the edge of the bed, and I pulled a chair up close.

His first question was, "Do you want to surrender to missions?"

"Nope, I sure don't," I replied.

"Why not?"

"Because I'll be sent to Africa and have to live all alone. I won't get to wear makeup, and I'll have to wear a black dress and put my hair in a bun. And, besides, I won't have a car."

Ted burst out laughing. "Hon, we have a big mission family. You'll have lots of friends. You can wear makeup and colored clothes. You can wear your hair any way you want, and we all have cars. Would it be okay if Pat and I prayed for your?" he asked.

"You can pray, but I'm still not going," I said and gave him my best scrunched up look.

"Fair enough," he said. "Oh, and what's your name?"

"Barbara. You can call me Barbi."

Ted began to pray. After two or three lines I interrupted. "Stop! Stop! I need to pray." Ted looked over at me and paused.

"Oh, God, I'm so miserable. I can't run away any longer. If you really want me to be a foreign missionary, I'll go. I want to be obedient."

I cried. Laughed. Released. And, oh, the joy and peace of surrender that poured over me!

Before I left, Ted and Pat hugged me and welcomed me to the mission family. It was easy to hug them back. My running was over, my anger was gone, and I was happy!

Later that evening, the last night of the World Missions Conference, I went to the front of the church and shared with the pastor my struggle and amazing day of surrender. He said, "Barbi, would you share this with our church now?"

I did, and with great joy.

I was 26 at the time. Except for the one year of Bible College I had never been to college. To prepare for missions, I needed to go to college and seminary. That was scary. School and studying had never been a priority for me. But with the support of my pastor and friends at First Baptist, Morristown, I applied to and was accepted at Carson-Newman College.

It wouldn't be fair to you if I didn't tell you what God did to supply the finances for college. I received several scholarships and a grant—not for academics, but for ministry.

For about three years, I had worked at a door/window and siding company. My plan was to continue to work until the day before orientation. That wasn't God's plan, though.

Three weeks before I was to leave the company, my boss came to speak to me. He stumbled over the words. "I hate to tell you this, because I know you need the money. The main office told me this morning they've decided to close this branch. Today is the last day. I don't understand because this branch is doing well."

"Today is my last day? Oh, boy, I was *not* expecting that," I said.

"Me either," he replied. "I can't tell you how sorry I am."

Now, here's the miracle of one way God provided for me. I had been determined to work three more weeks, but God closed the business that day. As a result, my income was deemed below the poverty level. If I had made five dollars more, I would have been thrown into a higher income bracket and had to forfeit my entire government grant.

God always knows best. I needed every minute of those three weeks to pack up and store things from my house, move to campus, and adjust to life in a dorm…living in half a room with a roommate.

During college, I became actively involved in any area that would help train me for mission work. For two summers I worked as a GA's and Acteens Camp Counselor. The next year, I was a summer missionary in Nashville, where I worked with internationals.

During my senior year in college, I served for two months in, of all places, the bush area of West Africa. Ha! Don't you know that God has a sense of humor? It was too hot to wear makeup; it melted down my face and slid off. Most of the time I wore a black, flowered sundress because it was lightweight. I wore my long hair in a bun because it was cooler that way. I didn't drive a car…but I did have a motorcycle. How fun!

While in seminary, I went on two mission trips to work with Native Americans in New Mexico.

God was getting me ready.

Yet even after seven years of higher education and all of the mission experiences, God had other plans. He closed the door to my becoming a career missionary. I was absolutely crushed.

For many years aftweward, I felt I had shamed my church in Tennessee. They had invested in me and generously helped me get through college; my Baptist Young Women's group had even paid for all my books for four years of school. I felt like I had failed them because I wasn't an overseas career missionary. It was a tremendous burden I carried for a long time.

Years later, I attended an International Mission Study at the church where my husband, James, pastored. The speaker said some are called to be foreign missionaries on a long-term career basis. But for others, the calling may be a career of short-term mission trips followed by sharing the story with others so that they might be encouraged to "go and do likewise."

Short-term mission trips. Yes! That's it! Finally, I understood God's purpose for my call. I hadn't failed my church after all.

Although the door to a long-term-missions career closed, God sent me to Russia to work in prisons and orphanages. I have since gone to Moldova twice, China twice, and also to Taiwan. On each of these trips, God provided opportunities to share the Gospel.

This has been my life. I have been obedient all along.

I'm free now. I know that I *am* a career missionary. All Christians are. Our lifestyle should be a career of missions telling people about Jesus, whether it's here or overseas. The location for our service is up to God! All we have to do is be obedient.

*BURKINA FASO,
WEST AFRICA
1983*

D'Antoni Took a Long Road to Africa

By Beth Harris

Reprinted from the Carson-Newman College Appalachian, 1983.

———◆———

Before I begin the stories of my time in Africa, I've included a yearbook article that Beth Harris, a student reporter, wrote about my time there. She brings out details from her interviews with me that I didn't write in my stories. Hope you enjoy it!

Monday, December 13, 1982
Dear Diary,
It was 9:30 A.M. I had to know whether I was going or not before Christmas break began this afternoon.
Riinnnnnnggggg!
"Hello, Barbi. This is Bill Henry. I'm just calling to let you know that you've been appointed to Upper Volta." [Now Burkina Faso, West Africa]
"Really, Bill? For sure—I really got it! Yippee! I can't believe it—wow! I just can't believe it. For sure?"
Needless to say, this was a wonderful day for me.
Love,
Barbi

Senior Barbi Dantoni was qualified to graduate two months before graduation. She finished the requirements for her degree on February 28, and on March 5 she was on her way to Sanwabo, Upper Volta, as a student missionary for two months.

A long road had led to the plane she boarded to fly to West Africa.

Her call to missions first came when she was a 12-year-old girl in Baltimore, Maryland. "Nobody would take me seriously because I was so young. But I kept on trying to tell people about Jesus. I was so excited about it, it turned a lot of them off—they called me Saint Barbara!"

But by the time she was 21, she didn't really want to be a missionary anymore, because "I thought a missionary wore black clothes and a bun in her hair and no makeup. I wasn't about to give up my makeup!"

God wasn't about to give up either. When she was 23, he brought her to Tennessee. She found a job and a church in Morristown and settled into doing sign language at her church as a way to fulfill her call. Then a World Missions Conference was held at the church. The tugging at her heart got so intense, she said, that she finally went to the hotel where Ted and Pat Cox, missionaries to Japan who were speaking at the conference, were staying. There she prayed. "Okay, Lord, I quit running! If you want me to be a missionary, I will."

Through members of the church, God provided money for her to enroll at CN. She started out majoring in psychology, but changed at the end of her first year to Individual Directions. "I didn't know why I was changing at the time, but later I looked back and realized that God's hand was in that change!"

The summer after her junior year brought another turning point, she said. "God allowed me to be chosen for summer missions. I worked with internationals. I could never have gone to Upper Volta if it hadn't been for that summer."

So the stage was set. In October 1982 she went to the state BSU Convention in Martin to speak about her experience as a summer missionary. She recalled the conversation she and God had when she heard about the semester student missions opportunities in Upper Volta at the convention. "God said, 'Why don't you do this?' and I said, 'God, I can't go to Africa! This is my year to graduate!' " But in adding up the pros and cons, she found the positive far outweighed the negative.

D'Antoni filled out the "multitudes of thousands of pages" of an application and then began to see if she could leave school for Africa in March. She found she could, and in December, the phone call came from Bill Henry, associate director of student ministries for the Tennessee Baptist Convention. She had been accepted.

She had only two months to get ready. In the second semester of her senior year, she had only ten hours left; if she'd had any more, she could not have finished in March. She filled the requirements with physical education courses and classes that were basically independent, such as Theological Research.

January and February were jammed. She took yellow fever, typhoid, DPT, cholera, and gammaglobulin shots; she swallowed malaria pills that she called "big pink M&Ms"; she got her passport; she went to orientation in Nashville; she tried to learn the Mooré language, which she would be teaching people to read and write in Sanwabo. Her time was so tightly scheduled, she laughed, that "when people came to see me, I almost asked, 'Do you have an appointment?' "

Because D'Antoni would have to take all the personal items she would need for two months in Sanwabo, the Campus Baptist Young Women had a "missionary shower" for her. Gifts included toothpaste, soap, sunscreen, film, and the gift she said was her favorite—12 rolls of toilet paper!

The Bible was a source of guidance and strength throughout the hectic semester, she said. A favorite verse of hers was a version of Philippians 4:13 that she learned in a Bible class here. "We went back to the original Greek and it said, 'I can **endure** all things through Christ who strengthens me.' "

When the time to leave came, she said, "I'm very happy inside. I'm going over there to give. My heart is in it, my soul, my spirit, my emotions, my whole being. This is what I've been preparing to do for four years."

She came back from the desertous country with a broader perspective, she felt. "When I first got there, I loved everything—I loved the world, I loved the people, I wanted to come back and live there.

"And then it hit me—I hate it, I hate this place, I hate everything. Lord, surely you don't want me in missions. You do not want me in this for the rest of my life!'

"I thought, 'There's a big mistake. I'm in the wrong vocation!' It was a shock. I was really angry with God about it, but I told Him I wasn't going to give up on Him.

"Then things started getting better. I didn't leave there fully knowing my call, but I know I'm still called to missions. I love my people there and my work. I hate the climate. But if God calls me back, I'll go."

She said the lifestyle of the people is "very primitive, very deprived, but yet they are very happy, and that seems to make up for the poverty. I don't think they realize how poor they are."

When she began teaching children to read and write in the Mooré dialect, she used only secular books. "But I felt convicted because I wasn't sharing with them, so then I brought my Bible and started teaching them Bible verses and games. Then I felt good about it.

"After working with my kids at Guenatenga (another village where she taught) for about six weeks, teaching them Bible verses and reading Bible stories in Mooré, one day they wanted to take my Bible home and read it to their village. So they did, and gathered all their people and read it. The next day, they told me how people had come out to listen to them. They were so proud of sharing the Gospel. That made the whole trip worthwhile!"

She found it nearly impossible to be alone. "There is no privacy anywhere in that whole country, I believe. If you want to cry, forget it unless you want everybody to hear," she said. "One day I had an upsetting day and so all the way back from Guenatenga, six miles away, I cried behind my dust mask and sunglasses on my moped. It was wonderful."

Other hardships included the heat, which reached as high as 130 degrees outdoors and 118 indoors, and drinking several glasses of uncooled water a day. D'Antoni emphatically said she had missed "ice cubes, milk, and chairs with a back." Then she added, "Spiritual food . . . and friends . . . and American church. But it really didn't take me that long to adjust, because I was expecting it to be a lot worse than it was."

Her sense of calling changed through the experience. "I

think my call over the last four years has been the dream part. Being a missionary is a respected career. But it's not above any other job, really. If God calls you to that, it doesn't make you any greater than anyone else. It's a gift, like any other gift. You can't idolize missions work. When I realized that, it freed me to be myself.

"It's hard—it's very hard. You have to be so flexible, and learning that was a step of growth for me. I need to be even more flexible, though, just like a spring."

Looking back over the rather unusual way she spent the last two months of her senior year, D'Antoni said, "I wasn't always happy. But I didn't have to be happy.—I just had to be there. It was more thorns than roses, but the payoff was people. If God calls me back, I'll go."

Having decided that, she felt, she could say in Mooré with her adopted people, "Laafi beeme—things are at peace."

Life in a Grass Hut

Burkina Faso, West Africa, 1983

No makeup! Hair in a bun! Wear black dresses! Go to Africa! *No Way*! At one time that was my opinion of a missionary's life, and that wasn't for me. Wouldn't you know it. God had other plans. Ten years later I found myself sweltering in the 126° temperatures of…guess where? Yes, West Africa. Upper Volta (now Burkina Faso), to be exact. My favorite outfit was a black sundress. Shaving my head would have been cooler, but I opted for a bun instead. The intense heat caused my makeup to run down my face, so I didn't wear any. Looking back, I now see that God really does have a marvelous sense of humor.

My home for two months was a six-foot by eight-foot grass hut with the luxury of a cement floor and a tin roof. A large straw door could be folded back for air and closed again for privacy. I also was one of two fortunate people to receive a single mattress on a wooden frame, instead of a canvas cot. None of our huts had electricity, but we did have lots of batteries and flashlights.

After arriving, as I checked out the straw construction of my new home, I heard a rustling sound over my head. I looked up just as a huge, ugly creature lost its grip from rafters, plopped down onto my neck, then fell to the floor.

"Yaaahhhh a dinosaur!" I screamed.

I ran out the opening of my hut and discovered a veteran missionary doubled over in laughter. "That," she struggled to speak as she gasped with laughter, "is a gecko. A lizard…*not* a dinosaur."

The creature was over a foot long, weighed about two pounds, had orange and black scales and a long spiked tail. I still think it was a baby dinosaur….

"Don't worry." She continued to laugh. "You'll get used to them."

"I don't think so," I told her.

"Yeah, it was bigger than usual," she replied as she tried not to grin.

After listening to tribal drums beat all night in addition to having jet lag, my brain was in a fog. To beat the crowd, I got up at 5 A.M. to shower and wash my hair. However, that quickly changed when I turned on the water. "Brrrr Hun-ga-wah!" I discovered the solar heated showers only gave hot water in the late afternoon! But I was definitely awake. As a newbie on the mission field, I now knew why no one waited in line to take a shower: You could get frostbite!

As Americans, we were privileged to have outhouses along with the shower room. The nationals did not. The outhouses weren't too bad, really, except for the 2 A.M. trips. I vividly remember one night as I was leaving the outhouse, I banged my toe on a door frame and dropped my flashlight into the "big hole." Total darkness. "Oh, no!" I gasped as visions of scorpions, spiders, and snakes immediately came to mind. Hallelujah! I didn't feel anything crawling on me and, praise the Lord, none found me!

Since the desert gets baking hot from 1:00-3:00 each afternoon, most people take a break. I was no exception. And it was *not* my favorite time of the day. Each day I stood in the shower fully clothed to soak myself and a towel. Next, I would lie down on my bed and cover myself from head to toe with the sopping towel. I did this not only to keep cool, but also to stop the flies from landing on my eyes to suck liquid from them. Swatting at the flies didn't help. They were fearless and thirsty, and eyes were great places for them to get hydrated. At the end of the two-hour break, my clothes, towel, and bed were completely dry. It was miserable and hot under the wet towel, but we did it to survive.

Since I was going to be living in a hut for two months, I attached a bright yellow stretchy clothesline from one straw wall to the other. In addition to using it to dry clothes, I had a section where I hung my photos.

In 1982, the movie *E.T. the Extra Terrestrial* was popular. I loved the movie, so I hung a photo of E.T. on my clothesline. I'll never forget the day one of my national friends, Ahngel (Angel), came to visit me. She clapped outside the straw door, which meant she wanted to enter. "*Beyella. Fo zindi Ka*" (Welcome. Sit down), I said. Angel looked around and saw the photo of E.T. Her eyes widened. She frowned and quickly looked over at me. I decided to prank her. I pointed to myself. "*Biiga*," (my child), I told her. She stared at the photo then she looked back at me and gave a quick nod. I think she felt sorry for me having such an ugly child. She never said a word, and neither did I. (Just so you know, I did ask God's forgiveness for playing this kind of joke and never correcting it.)

Hut living is challenging. Forget privacy. Our huts were built on a single cement slab long enough to accommodate maybe ten huts. The only thing that divided the huts were the straw walls in between. Definitely not sound proof.

We had a generator at the mission compound for the camp refrigerator and stove. It ran from 7 A.M. to 11 P.M. each day. It was loud, but if you fell asleep before 11, you might get some rest before all the snoring started. In hut life every sneeze, cough, or banging of a suitcase is heard…by everyone.

Another interesting fact I discovered was how cold it got around 2 A.M. The temperature went down to about 90˚. In the desert, that's cold. I used two wool blankets each night but had to toss them by 5 A.M. when the sun came up because it was hot again.

The one day I'll never forget was when Boofer, the vet's monkey, hustled over the walls of my hut and landed on me. I was sitting on my bed writing a letter when my grass walls started to shake. Boofer hopped over and made himself comfy on my lap. His jaws were smacking up and down. His yellow teeth chomped and chewed. Somehow he had gotten into a teammate's suitcase and stolen bubble gum. Fascinated, I watched his mouth contort in shapes I didn't think possible. Suddenly he grabbed my blouse and ripped it open.

"Oh, my! Oh, my! Boofer, what are you doing?"

He searched my skin looking for fleas. I didn't have any. That did not make him happy. In monkey world, it is polite to de-flea each other and eat the evidence. Since I didn't reciprocate, he furiously scolded me and exited my hut.

I do believe I was in shock. Half of my clothes had been

ripped apart by a bubble-gum-chewing monkey. I was expected to pick off and eat fleas, and all I did was scream and get scolded. "Ahh, the adventures of hut life."

Scorpions, scorpions, scorpions. There are all sizes of scorpions. They are sneaky and like to hide in dark, cozy places like inside shoes, under the bed covers, and behind luggage. Of course, the brave ones might run across the room or over your foot. Each night by flashlight, I had to strip my bed, shake out the covers then remake it. In addition, I always gave my shoes a good shaking before putting them on.

The world encourages us to be positive and keep looking up, but in the bush of West Africa, it's wiser to look down, around, then up. Chances of survival are better.

We could keep snacks in our hut. But it was quite a task getting to them. I put nuts and raisins in a zip-lock bag inside of another zip-lock bag inside of a plastic bag. Then, I put them in a plastic container with a lid, put that inside another bag, and placed them in my trunk. Grrrr! Ants still got in!

Whether or not you retrieved the snack showed how desperate you were. I learned from some of the long-termers you could give the bag a good shake and the ants would get confused and try to exit. After the shaking, you had to brush them off and then eat your snack. I tried the technique a few times, but I decided it was gross.

One of the key words at the mission compound was "flexibility." I kept big rubber bands on my nightstand as a reminder!

What about décor in a grass hut? Since I was going to be there two months, I tried to make my hut cozy. I had a blue trunk, my yellow-flowered bed cover from college, a side table, the yellow clothesline with photos, and a red plastic lantern. I also had a live tree. Neat, huh? The tenant before me had expanded the back walls of the hut to enclose the only tree in the compound. I loved it.

The camp nurse shared the tree with me because she lived beside me and the wall of her hut had also been expanded. We couldn't decide what to call our bonus space. It wasn't a patio or a porch. It was just a bigger space, in the sand, with a tree; but it did give us sunlight, and that made hut life easier in the daytime for the two of us. It also meant our huts weren't as hot as the enclosed huts because we had airflow.

There was one rule that everyone had to follow or be sent home immediately: Wear shoes at all times, even in the shower. Conditions are primitive in the bush. There are no public toilets. The nationals believed that when nature calls, you should not hold it because it's not good for your health. Therefore, wherever you are may also become your toilet area. We were warned that if we went barefooted, most likely we'd get diseases or worms. Parasites are tiny; you can't even see them, but they easily enter the foot and spread throughout the body. We were required to wear shoes until getting into bed or onto our cots.

Thankfully, flip flops worked well in the hut and showers.

You may wonder if I'd live in a grass hut again. Yes, I think so. It was challenging and hard at times, but it was also an amazing experience.

How about you? Would you try hut life?

My hut is the one between the poles.

Inside my hut with the tree in the back

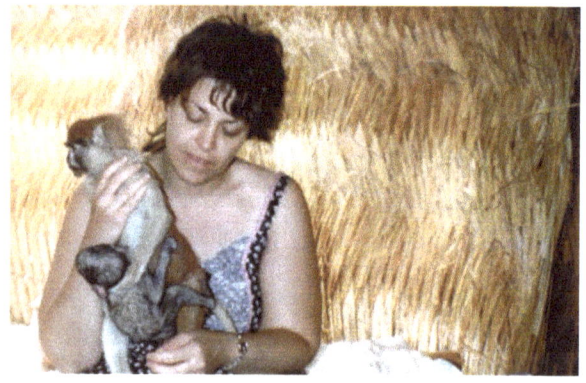

In my hut with BJ (the big monkey)
and Boofer (the smaller monkey)

Motorcycle Mama

Burkina Faso, West Africa, 1983

My first motorcycle lesson took place on an old airstrip in Upper Volta, West Africa. Melba, my teacher, showed me how to rev up the engine, kick the stand, and use the hand brake. *Varrrooommmmm.* Before she finished speaking I accidentally turned the throttle…and off I went. Melba jumped back, then watched in horror as I began to steer toward her. She started running. With hair blowing, elbows pumping, and dirt flying, she ran as fast as she could. Still, it appeared I was going to mow her down!

"Hellllpp!" I yelled. "Ohhhh! What do I do? What do I do?"

"Use the brake! Left hand," she gasped.

I slid to a halt. "Whoa! Whew!" I muttered. Once my heart slowed down, I grinned. "That really was kind of fun!"

Panting and wiping sweat from her face, Melba squinted in sternness and puffed, "Next time, use the brake…sooner!"

I had no time to practice my new skill. At seven the next morning I'd begin my trek across the desert to the village of Guanatenga (Juh na tenga), where I was to teach literacy classes in Mooré. The teacher whose place I was taking told me our village was six miles away. "Be sure and follow my bike exactly," she said. "If you go out of the ruts in the sand, you'll wreck your motorcycle."

On my second day of motorcycle mania, I donned a skirt and blouse, headscarf, sunglasses, bright blue knapsack, and a dust mask. Instead of motorcycle mama, I looked more like motorcycle monster!

I wondered what the African nationals thought.

After driving six times a week for over a month, I got overconfident in my motorcycle skills. I decided to speed up a bit. Not a good choice. Driving in the sandy desert was not easy.

In the bush there were a few rules to remember whether on land or on a motorcycle: 1) *Always* greet or wave to *everyone* you meet. 2) Use *only* your right hand for everything; the left hand is used in place of toilet paper. 3) Women must wear dresses and *never* show their knees. Sounds simple, right? Ha! Just try to apply those rules while driving a motorcycle!

Sadly enough, following the rules and getting a bit careless and over-confident caused me to have a bike accident. A man walked close by and waved just as I took a sharp left turn in an area where the narrow path in the sand wasn't clear. Of course, I was required to wave back. That presented a problem. I had to use my right hand, which also controlled the gas. Then my skirt blew up showing my knees. He stared. Trying to get my skirt down and give the motorcycle more gas, I lost control and wiped out.

*Plop, kurplunk, thump…*I came out of the rut.

My face slid in the sand, which went up my nose and into my mouth. The motorcycle cut off and landed on top of me.

Stunned, I laid there in silence.

"Ughh, ooohh. That hurt." I shook a few body pieces and parts. Nothing seemed broken, so I tried to crawl out from under the bike.

When motorcycles aren't moving and are on top of you, they are quite heavy. I clawed around in the sand and inched my way from underneath. Things were blurry, and I was having trouble breathing. I gave a few hard snorts and blew the sand out of my nose. Then I did a couple of spits to get the sand out of my mouth. If I hadn't hurt so much, I would have laughed. Now I looked like a dusty, sand-breathing dragon, instead of a monster.

Groaning, I looked at the gash in my arm and then up at the curious faces and outstretched hands all eager to shake my hand and bid me, "*Laafi Beeme*."

"Oh, no!" Where in the world had the multitudes come from? There were no trees, huts, roads—only the barren desert—and, yet, there were over 50 people standing there staring at me. For over 45 minutes, I stood there, shook each outstretched hand and gave the expected *Laafi Beeme* greeting. Finally, I slowly climbed back on "the Beast" to head to the village.

Arriving at the village, I was surprised to see my students running toward me. They weren't happy and pointed to the sun, then back at me. I was late and they knew it. But, how did they know? No one had a watch.

They knew because the sun moved and the shadows were different. Now I understood.

Denis, an 11-year-old student, pointed to my bloody shoulder. "Ooh, ooh, ooh! *Karemsamba*" (teacher), he said. I looked at my right arm near the shoulder and saw an oval gash over two inches long. The gash was bleeding a lot. Blood was running down my arm.

Oh, dear, I'm wounded more than I thought.

The next thing I knew my precious students had gathered around, patting my arm, rubbing my back, and touching my hair to show me their comfort and love. It was hard not to cry from these tender actions. But, in their culture tears weren't acceptable, so I held them back.

After class, I headed back to the mission compound.

Did you know when the sun moves across the sky, the desert path also changes? I didn't. Until it happened to me.

It was easy to get lost because there were no street signs, no streets, no traffic lights, no landmarks. The shadows had changed, and nothing looked familiar. I almost panicked. *Oh, God, help! Help!* I prayed.

He did. God loves to bless His children. In His sweet mercy, He guided and directed my path in the desert and got me safely home.

My heart gave many thanks that day.

It is a good thing to give thanks unto the Lord, and to sing praises unto thy name, O most High. (Psalm 92:1 KJV)

Baarka Wennaam (Thank you, God).

Motorcycle Mama before the accident

In my hut holding Jenene, Angel's biiga
(child) after the motorcycle accident

The Chief's Finery

Burkina Faso, West Africa, 1983

In the bush area of Burkina Faso, I learned that it was extremely prestigious to own underclothes. If a person owned a piece of underclothing, they were greatly honored and respected by their tribesmen.

It also caused a lot of jealousy, and one might be challenged to give up their treasure.

Needless to say, we Americans had several pairs of all kinds of undergarments with us. When the wash boy hung them on the line to dry, they were often stolen. In fact, we quickly learned to lock our underthings in our trunks. (Our open grass huts were easily accessible.) Otherwise, because of the cultural value of "what is yours is mine, and what is mine is yours," our underclothing could easily become shared community property.

Imagine my surprise and, at first, embarrassment when I saw African nationals wearing the prestigious underwear on the outside of their clothing. How to wear some of the pieces was a bit confusing to the villagers. For example, bras, slips, and men's briefs were often worn backwards or inside out. But my, my, did it ever raise peer esteem to be seen in underwear!

For me, the most surprising moment came during one Sunday morning church service. With his arms crossed over his chest, one of the village chiefs pranced regally down the aisle and sat on the front bench. He was sweating profusely as he paraded his finery—a toasty, set of thermal long johns. It was 126° and sweltering hot, but this was his moment of glory. Not only did the chief have underwear, but it was the ultimate set of underwear: a long-sleeved top and a full-legged bottom! Surely, this elevated both the chief and the people to a more noble status and gave the village of Sanwabo a higher regard among the other village tribes.

The procession was stately as he strutted in his regalia. We Americans were aghast and tried not to chuckle.

However, when I learned the significance of underwear to them, I saw that indeed history had been made. At first, my cultural filter had been distorted. Once I learned the meaning, I could rejoice in the victory and enjoy his success.

Nevertheless, I continued to keep my underclothes in a safe place.

They All Wore White

Burkina Faso, West Africa, 1983

T**HE SUN BEGAN POKING ITS HEAD OUT AT** 5:18 A.M. By six it was fully awake and casting magnificent rays of warmth over the tiny village of Sanwabo. It was Easter Sunday, 1983. What a glorious day it was to be for the Christians of the Mossi Tribe!

I'll never forget that Sunday. Christians traveled for days by foot through scorching desert regions of Africa to participate in worship. It was to be a day sharing scriptures, songs, and three-hour sermons. It was a time of rejoicing because Mossi Christians had learned that Christ was resurrected 2,000 years ago. Many were new believers. They knew that, today, Christians all over the world would share the same celebration. The Mossi also wanted to celebrate Christ.

In a land where voodoo and sorcery were known ways of life, Mossi Christians wanted to make a proclamation about their new-found faith in Jesus Christ. They decided to wear white on Easter Sunday. In a poverty-stricken, third-world country, this almost was an impossibility. There was no money to buy material.

There were no nearby markets to purchase clothing. Water was scarce for drinking; to bathe or wash clothes was a luxury. Yet, God provided! My friends of the village willingly sacrificed meager belongings to get white garments to demonstrate their love for Christ.

How could I show them I, too, loved Christ? When I had packed to make the trip to Africa, I knew white would be hard to keep clean, so I had only taken colored clothes.

I remembered seeing a white nightgown in a storage area of the camp. I could wear the nightgown as a blouse and put a skirt over the bottom! In America I would have been scorned if I'd ventured to church in such an outfit! In Africa my pride had to be sacrificed. It was more important to be identified as a believer in Christ than to parade the simple Easter finery I had brought with me.

As the sun rose, we could hear the sound of tribal singing. Hundreds of tired and hungry Christians climbed over the many sand dunes of the desert. The sun reflected off their white garments flapping in the dusty breezes. Their eyes radiated the pure joy of being a child of God. Members of our compound ran to welcome our guests and bring greetings. They knew me instantly, not by name or face, but by my white nightgown! They ran toward us, exchanging handshakes and the customary greeting of *Laafi Beeme*, "Things are at peace."

What a celebration we had! We sang, worshipped, ate, and did it all over again. I learned so much that day: In whatever part of the world, when Christians meet, there is fellowship and a spiritual bond. These beloved people worshipped Christ with everything in them. They had traveled for three days across the barren desert to worship with believers from across the land and world.

What love! What sacrifice! What joy!

What an example of a Christ-follower! What a blessing to me!

Oh, to be more like the Mossi....

Dear Ones, may your fellowship be sweet as you meet other Christians along the way.

They Understood

Burkina Faso, West Africa, 1983

My school building was a one-room hut that also served as the worship house on Sundays. The straw building was 5 feet tall and about 12 feet wide.

My seat was a tire rim turned on its side. Therefore, I balanced myself on the tire rim while I held a book in one hand and a piece of chalk in the other hand. My blackboard, about 3 feet tall by 4 feet long, was scarred and chipped with a lot of holes throughout. There were no desks, so the students sat in a circle on the sand.

Since I was 5 feet 7 inches tall, it was impossible to stand up in my classroom for long. When I did stand to emphasize a point, my head crashed against the roof or went through the one ventilation hole at the top.

On one occasion, the students called out *"Karemsamba, Karemsamba"* (teacher, teacher) and excitedly pointed to the roof.

I looked up. "Oh, my." There stood a camel gnawing on the straw roof. This was exciting, so all of us hurried out to see it. The owner of the camel made gestures, and the students told me he wanted me to ride the camel. I had ridden a camel in Israel, but that had been 10 years earlier. I tried to motion to the man I had no *ligdi* (money). He insisted I ride. Down the camel came and up the teacher went. The kids cheered, and I held on. After walking us around a while, the man stopped, the camel got on its knees, and I climbed off as modestly as I could in a dress. I loved it! The man waved goodbye, and we went back in to finish class.

We didn't accomplish much during the last hour. The kids laughed and talked. I never knew what they said, but I think I passed some kind of bravery test.

Another day a stray lamb walked into our classroom. This time, I was the one pointing and hollering, "Oh, oh, oh!" The kids were not impressed. Apparently this was a common occurrence. But my brain sang "Mary had a little lamb, little lamb, little lamb…." It was a great nursery-rhyme moment for this tired teacher perched on her uncomfortable tire rim.

One day, Paseba, a beautiful, shy 10 year old, brought me a gift. In America, we think of giving an apple to the teacher. I didn't receive an apple. I received a treasured and costly gift of three raw eggs. Previously someone had told me that eggs were a gift of friendship and acceptance. I graciously accepted my gift and thanked her. She looked up at me and gave me a big smile.

Now I had a dilemma. How would I get them home on a motorcycle? There was a strong possibility the eggs were rotten. Paseba wouldn't have known that, but I did. If I put them in my knapsack and they broke during the rough ride, all my teaching materials would be ruined. I did the only thing I could think of. I tucked my blouse snuggly into my skirt, took off my head scarf, wrapped the eggs in it, and nestled them inside my blouse on my stomach. The kids nodded their approval. In a culture where few clothes are worn, my actions of stuffing eggs down my blouse was not embarrassing or disrespectful to the students. They considered it a wise decision.

Let me tell you, I drove carefully during my six-mile journey. When I didn't need to use both hands, I cradled my left hand on top of my nesting eggs and prayed they wouldn't break. I drove straight to the screened-in dining room and entered the kitchen. Frieda, the cook, looked at me clutching my stomach and rushed over.

"Are you okay? Are you ill?" she asked.

"Nope. I come bearing a gift of eggs." I laughed and reached down my blouse to pull out the nest.

Frieda told me we'd do a float test on the eggs. "If they sink, they're fresh. If they float, they might be bad," she said.

All three eggs floated. We decided not to eat them. Still, Paseba's gift was given in love, and that meant a lot to me.

One of the highlights of my time in Africa came unexpectedly a week before I was to leave. My students begged me to allow them to take the Mooré Bible home to read to the villagers. It was one of our two textbooks. I was suspicious of the request, since owning a book was impressive, and almost unheard of.

"*Ai yo, ai yo*" (no, no), I said as I shook my head.

They motioned yes to me, over and over. Through gestures, they promised to keep it safe and bring it back. After class, I carefully wrapped it in my headscarf and handed it over.

Will I ever see our Bible again?

Arriving at the village school the next morning, I was surprised to see my students running and shouting, with their arms flailing the air. "*Karemsamba! Karemsamba!*" they shouted.

They crowded around me and tried to talk all at once. "We read about Jesus dying on the cross and His resurrection. He is alive, and our village understood us! Hallelujah Amen!"

I clapped and clapped. "*Karembiisi* (students), *yaa soma, yaa soma*" (good, good). With great love and respect, I looked at each one of my precious students and smiled. I was so proud of them. They had become missionaries to their own village!

The day before my last class, I told the students we would have a party the next day. "Can anyone bring a drum?" I asked. Several boys shook their head, yes.

When I drove up to class the next morning, my students ran out of the hut to greet me. They looked at my stuffed knapsack and giggled. It wasn't flat like usual.

All the kids got comfy on the sand floor, and I opened my knapsack. They leaned forward to peek. I pulled out a bottle of the famous orange Yuki drink. "Oooh." Then I pulled out a second bottle. "Ahh." Claps followed this one. I handed out cups and had Paseba pour the drinks. Then I pulled out fruit bars and candy. Their eyes lit up in delight, and I was rewarded by big smiles. We munched and talked. Rather, they talked, and I tried to understand a few words.

"Let's sing," I suggested. Always thrilled to have music, the guys scrambled to get the drums they had placed in the corner. We sang and swayed to the beat of the tribal worship songs. It was fun.

"*Karemsamba*," I said and pointed to myself and a drum. Wen-pang-go handed me his drum. We sang "J Z Zak a-man," my favorite song. I joyfully tapped out the rhythm.

"*Karemsamba, ai yo, ai yo*" (Teacher, no, no). Wen-pang-go shook his head rapidly and took back his drum. I understood the message. My heart was in it, but I just didn't possess the talent to play an African drum. I gave my best pouty face, and we all had a hearty laugh.

At the end of class, I gave each child a pencil, some paper and a piece of candy to take with them. I sighed. This was my final visit with my beloved students. I couldn't hold back the tears this time. Oh, I loved these kids.

"*Ai yo, ai yo, Karemsamba.*" They pointed to my tears and shook their heads.

I wiped my eyes, took a big gulp, and smiled.

Before I left, I prayed with them. We put our hands on top of each other. The kids were somber. This time I prayed the whole prayer, with the exception of a few English words, in complete Mooré. After the amen, the kids looked up. Now they had tears in their eyes.

"*Poh-tiri, Karemsamba, poh-tiri*" (We understand, Teacher, we understand).

I had thought the children reading the Bible in their village was the highlight of my trip. No, this was the highlight. God helped me pray in their language, and they understood me.

I hugged each child goodbye and told them I loved them. Then I reminded them God loved them, too.

The heat, the scorpions, the motorcycle wreck was all worth it for this one, priceless moment. They understood my heart and my prayer for them. They received my blessing upon them. All six miles back to the compound, I cried. I wailed. I grieved. This time I wouldn't hold it back.

God, you are good. Thank you for my Karembiisi (students). Amen.

J Z Zak a-man

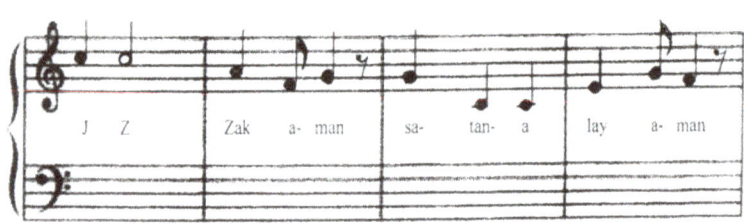

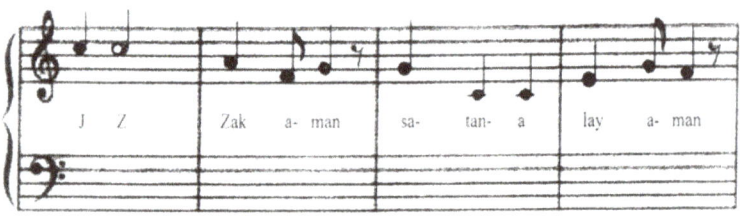

Translation: "Jesus Christ is risen, satan is defeated. Alleluia!"
A village, tribal song from the Sanwabo area; words and tune as remembered by Barbara D'Antoni Diggs.

RUSSIA
1993

A Little Kindness Goes a Long Way

Russia, 1993

"Why don't you go to Russia with us in January?" asked Dr. Anderson.

"Hah! For free?"

"The cost is $2,000 and you need to raise your own support," he replied and handed me an application. Dr. Anderson was the director of the Southwestern Baptist Theological Seminary's World Mission and Evangelism Center (WMEC). He was one of my former professors and someone I had known for 10 years.

In 1992, I was contracted by the Women's Missionary Union to write a curriculum article about a couple serving as missionaries in Kazakstan, a former Soviet Republic state. I knew nothing about the country. Since I lived near Southwestern Seminary, I had walked over to the campus and into the WMEC to do research.

At home, I glanced at the application, and then tossed it into the trash. It would be a great experience, but, me go to Russia? Impossible.

During the next week I thought a lot about going to Russia.

In fact, I even dreamed about it. "James, you know it might be possible for me to go on this trip after all." My husband stared at me like I was crazy. "I feel led to pursue this."

He shook his head, "Barbara, it's November 7, and $2,000 is a lot of money to get in a short time." He did, however, agree that I should pursue it until God closed the doors.

At nine the next morning, I was back at the WMEC. I confessed to throwing away the first application and asked for another.

Walking home, I felt God tell me to start preparing. I thought about a list of clothes I would need, supplies to take and teaching materials. I also planned a list of frozen meals to prepare for James while I was gone to Russia.

"God, what's next?"

I felt Him lead me to write a few letters to people about this trip possibility. Prayers to make the right decision were my main concern. God led me to write only one line about the need for financial support. The letters were written and mailed right after lunch. Next, came a list of Russian words I hoped to learn.

Three days after I mailed my letters, I received a long-distance phone call. The caller and his wife had hoped to contribute money for a church member going to Russia, but the Lord already had supplied the man's need. They were disappointed, but then my letter arrived! They knew the money was to go to me. The caller said, "The only reason we are sending $1,000 and not the whole amount is so others can share in the blessing."

"Oh, and I am sending you a blank check," the donor continued. "Whatever you don't get, just fill it in. If you don't go to Russia, it won't be for lack of money."

I was speechless. Then I cried, laughed, kissed the dogs, and shouted, "Doggies, I'm going to Russia!" *Oh God, thank you. This is truly a miracle.*

The best part of the miracle, though, was watching for James to return home from work. As soon as I saw him walk down the driveway, I ran to meet him and share the news. "James! Guess what? I'm going to Russia!"

"Yeah, right," he said.

"No. It's true I'm going!"

"Do you have the finances?" He asked as he opened the door and sat on the sofa.

"Yes, I do. God provided!" I told him about the phone call.

"Wow! Wow! Oh, wow!" my quiet husband then burst out.

I loved it. It was wonderful watching him share the joy with me. We hugged and hugged.

Finally, in sheer reverence he managed, "This *really* is God at work!"

Yes, it did look like I was going to Russia! Within days, money started coming in from everywhere: $800, $500, $100, $50, $25, $15, $8…. People were very bighearted, and I was overwhelmed by the generosity shown to me. My prayer was, *Lord, I dedicate all this money and myself to you. Please use me, so that I might lead others to know you. There is so much to do in Russia and so little time. Please help me do what's right. Amen.*

God was faithful and provided enough money to cover my expenses and to purchase everything I needed for the trip. In fact, I begged people not to give me any more money. I guess God knew best, though, because it kept coming. With the extra money, I was able to help Christians in Russia and also leave money for the church in St. Petersburg.

"To Russia with Love" became the theme for the last two months of 1992 at the Diggs' household in Ft. Worth, Texas. While hectic and, at times, frantic, how exciting it was to prepare for another mission venture that would change my life! I had to buy wool socks, waterproof boots, earmuffs, heavy gloves, long underwear, and gifts of trail mix, candy, and tea for new Russian friends. I also needed to prepare Bible lessons, get vaccinations, and apply for visas, not to mention celebrate Christmas, attend parties, pack, study Russian and cook meals to leave behind for James. Our guest room looked more like a street market. Surely, anything one needed was strewn about this mini "Russian" room.

Finally, the day arrived. At 4 A.M. my husband helped me bundle up in *all* those winter clothes: three pairs of socks, two pairs of long underwear, slacks, a dress to wear over the slacks, two sweaters plus a turtleneck, boots, gloves, scarf, and coat. It appeared I was dressed for a hike in the snow in Siberia, not for an airplane ride.

Our team gathered at the seminary, had prayer, then headed to the airport.

Settled in the plane, it wasn't long before I was overheated and sweating profusely. I had on so many clothes I barely fit in the airplane seat. Finally, I got up and went to the lavatory to see what clothing I could remove. Have you ever tried to get out of hiking boots and peel off a set of long underwear in an airplane bathroom? Brutal. Nevertheless, it did cool me off some. Next, the challenge was getting six pieces of clothing into my stuffed carry on. I did it, but my flexible bag barely fit back into the overhead rack.

Thirty-six hours after leaving home, including a five-hour layover in Finland, we arrived in Russia. What a shock! Our plane landed in the middle of a dark and rainy airfield. There were no buildings around us, no other planes, no gates, no lights, just us and vast grayness. KGB holding rifles, wearing black fur caps and long overcoats stood outside our plane. After almost an hour, they allowed us to leave the plane, but told us not to speak and to keep our eyes forward.

The metal steps exiting the plane were damaged and wobbled. There were no safety slats, only hand rails. The steps were slick and covered with patches of ice. I tried to hold to the railing, but it was also frozen. Several times I nearly slid off the steps. No one assisted us. The KGB stood like statues, yet their piercing, watchful eyes slowly followed our every move.

We heard a loud rattling and smelled gasoline. Across the airstrip, came a dirty, snow-encrusted shuttle bus. The driver climbed out, jerked his thumb toward the door and uttered one word, "in."

We looked around at the isolation and wondered where he would take us. We threw our heavy carry-on bags inside the door and climbed up the steep steps. Then we were driven to a rundown terminal.

The terminal was almost deserted. An occasional light bulb swung from a wire in the ceiling. The fixtures were worn and shabby, and the few seats scattered around had ripped upholstery. The workers hunched over their counters. Still, no one talked, and no one smiled. It was an eerie feeling to be in such gloom.

Our group got our baggage and trudged towards Customs and Immigration in the airport terminal. I was a bit nervous because the passport with my identification, medicines, and tickets were all in my maiden name. I hadn't had time to get them changed before getting my visa. I also used my old driver's license. Hopefully, I wouldn't slip and put my married name on my debarkation form.

I was close to the back of the customs line. So far, the luggage of every one of the other team members had been thoroughly torn apart and searched.

While in Greece, 20 years before this, I had spoken two Greek words at a 3 A.M. customs check-in and was allowed to go right through. If I spoke a little Russian, would it work for me again?

I took a deep breath. *"Zdrastvuyte, dobriy vyercher."* (Hello, good evening), I said.

The man in the customs booth squinted, and looked up at me. Then he dropped his head. I thought I'd better try another word. The only thing I could think of was, *Kak vas zavut?"* (What is your name?)

The man grinned and lifted his eyes. "You speak Russian very well."

"I do?"

Then he asked, "What else can you say?"

"Maybe 10 or more phrases."

"What are they?" he challenged.

Dobraye utra (good morning); *dobriy dyen* (good afternoon); *da svidenya* (good-bye); *spakoynay nochi* (good night); *kak dila?* (how are you?); *minya zavut* (my name is); *pazhalsta* (please or you're welcome); *spasiba* (thank you); *skolka stoit?* (how much?); *gdye toulet?* (where is the toilet?); and *chay se limonom* (tea with lemon).

He smiled. "Very good, you need to learn more of the language," and punched his partner to make sure he agreed.

"*Dah.*" His partner's head nodded up and down.

The man who had challenged my Russian told me to go on through the line.

I hesitated. "Don't you want me to open my bags?"

"*Nyet.*" He shook his head and grinned. "You speak Russian; go on through."

I gave him a big smile. *Just like in Greece. Knowing and speaking some of the language once again got me through customs. Thank you, God.*

Ahead of us stood a huge group of people squashed into the corner behind a roped barrier. This intrigued me. I got the attention of one of the women, smiled and waved. She waved back and held up a sign that identified her as our tour leader. She and the group of people were waiting for us. The folks in the corner were from the Temple of the Gospel church in St. Petersburg. What a sight for our weary eyes!

"*Slava Boga*, the Americans are here," they cheered and clapped. "Our Christian brothers and sisters have come!"

They had come to bring us greetings in Christ's name. As we stepped closer, eyes lit up, mouths broke into toothy grins and arms reached out to hug us close. These dear, dear people had walked in the cold and rain for hours to get to their church, and then they endured a rough, two-hour bus ride to the airport. They stood, not sat, for many hours and waited for us to arrive.

The Soviet Union under Communist rule had collapsed two years earlier. Christianity and the freedom to worship meant everything to these Russian believers. Now fellow Christians had come across the ocean to teach, train, and worship with them. Most of the people were elderly, yet they sacrificed to come to the airport to be sure we felt welcomed. Oh, yes, we felt not only welcomed, but also loved, cherished, and united in Christ. My eyes fill with tears.

I remember it so well. It is as if I am again in the airport with them.

We were on the shuttle for two hours after leaving the airport. Traveling was difficult and we were exhausted, but we also were curious to observe our new surroundings. My first impression of Russia was that everything looked the same: massive, with battleship-grey cement buildings. Many of the barren and aged buildings looked like dilapidated sanitariums that held deep dark secrets within their walls.

An empty and desolate feeling hung over us.

I sighed. *Would we ever arrive at our hotel?* We turned the corner. *Whoa!* There it was. Our hotel looked intimidating. Almost three blocks in length, it looked like a huge, cement prison, definitely not a luxury hotel. The inside was not what I expected either. No windows lined the lobby or corridors. The carpets were red and threadbare, and some of the room numbers hung half-off the doors. It was not a welcome sight, and it took forever to get to our rooms. I'm sure we walked two blocks from the entrance to our rooms.

There were rules to follow in Russian hotels. To get to our rooms, each guest was required to first check in with the key lady on their floor. She verified our information then gave us our room key. We had to return the key when leaving the room. No exceptions. These gruff, stolid women guarded the keys for their floor and acted like hotel security, housekeepers, and nurses. They watched everything. Unfortunately, key ladies also unlocked the doors when we weren't there and tended to browse or pilfer items of interest. Therefore, each day I repacked and locked everything back into my suitcase.

The most unusual thing I noticed about the hotel was all the cats walking the corridors. They seemed right at home and acted like they had lived there all their nine lives. I later learned the cats roamed the halls to catch mice.

Good job, kitties. Keep up the good work!

After putting my suitcase in the room, I opened my door as our two seminary professors passed by. They waited for me to catch up and together we walked down the hall to supper. Two women wearing heavy makeup stood in the hallway and followed us. Next, they openly propositioned the professors. Both the professors and I ignored them and continued walking. That didn't go over well. The women screamed something ugly and spit at me. *Surely, they don't think I'm a threat to their business.*

We rounded the corner and the three of us got into an elevator the size of a small closet. Our arms were pinned to our sides and our noses almost touched. Ugh. We felt the vibrations and heard the grinding of the rusted chains as the antiquated elevator started to move.

Then it happened. The elevator jolted and hesitated between floors. Then it made a screeching sound and shook before it came to a stop. There was no emergency button, light, soft music, or ventilation, only darkness. It was already tight in there; now it felt like the walls were squeezing in on us. My breathing came out in rapid puffs. The professors began to gulp for air as well.

We beat on the doors. Our hot breath slapped each other in the face as we yelled for help. No one came. It was stuffy, hot, hard to breathe. We shouted and pounded again. All of our cries for help echoed off the walls.

One of the professors spoke, "You're not claustrophobic are you, Barbara?"

My heart raced and I grabbed an arm. "Uh, huh."

"Don't panic!" he said. "Don't panic."

Little did that professor know, *don't panic* was the message I was already giving myself.

My mind went into rapid overdrive, and I had horrific visions of "the stranded elevator trio" being carried out as upright corpses. Our tombstones would read, "They came to do mission work, but suffocated in the elevator trying to get to their first supper."

After what seemed like hours, but in reality was only 15 long minutes, the elevator vibrated and plunged downward. Once again, I grabbed an arm and started gasping for air. A man outside the elevator banged and hammered on the doors, and with a loud creak, he pried them open. I couldn't get out fast enough. The professors were right behind me. We sucked in stale air that smelled of cigar smoke, wiped the sweat off our faces, huddled together, and prayed. "Oh, God, thank you. Thank you."

Then we ventured down several levels of dark tunnel ramps to the underground dining room. It felt like we were entering a dungeon. But we had arrived at last!

The gray room resembled a tomb that attempted to boast an ancient elegance. The walls were enormous cement blocks with ornate Russian carvings. It was dark except for a few light sconces on the walls that reflected off the white linens covering each table. Unmatched pieces of china and clear tea glasses were on the tables. Each plate of food for the event was the same: a thin slice of beef, a boiled potato, black caviar, and a slice of pickle. Waiters, their faces showing no emotion, stood dressed in shabby tuxedoes. Emotionless waitresses were next to them in black dresses. Again, no one smiled or spoke. It was like being in a roomful of robots.

My inexpressible joy came later when, in Russian, I thanked a waitress for pouring my tea. She dipped her head and a smile softened her face. With a nod she responded, "*Pazhalsta*" (You're welcome). That was all I needed. I tried out all 17 of my Russian phrases on anyone who came near me. It felt wonderful to thank people for the sincere kindnesses they showed us. My smiles and attempts at the language seemed to make a difference to them, too. My robot-like servers became human again. They stood straighter, took time to smile often and looked for me at the following meals. It seemed a little kindness goes a long way, even on the other side of the world.

In the days ahead, I continued to learn the truth of this statement.

Nadia Helped Change Lives

Russia, 1993

D ETERMINED, ALERT, STEADFAST, strong, sensitive, and searching for knowledge. This was Nadia. She sat over in the corner of the room with the professors discussing the strategy for the mission team's schedule. Yet, every few minutes she turned her head to look over at me. Her eyes squinted and her brow creased, then she would shyly smile. I knew she was trying to fit something together, but I wasn't sure what it was.

As soon as the professors finished the conversation, Nadia stood and headed toward me. I made my way in her direction.

"I think I must know you," she said. "Have we met before?"

"No, we've never met. This is my first time in Russia, and I've never seen you before."

She hesitated. "But you look so familiar."

Grinning and nodding my head I said, "I know why we look familiar to each other. It is because you see Jesus in me and I see Jesus in you. It is His spirit that's familiar. We are sisters in the Lord."

"Yes. That must be it!" she exclaimed. "We are sisters."

Immediately, a tremendous spiritual bond formed. Over the next 13 days it was to grow even stronger.

Nadia, our interpreter, had been a Christian for two years. During her teens and twenties, she served as an officer in the Communist Youth League. Now she was serving the one true God, Jesus Christ. She was eager to know more about Him.

On one particular day, Nadia took us to the hospital. Our nearly-frozen team trudged into the stifling building, so typical of Russia. Thawing quickly, we soon wished for a breath of cool air.

The hospital was shabby and reeked of unpleasant odors. Despite the smell and lack of furniture, it looked surprisingly well-scrubbed and clean. The long hallways were dark and uninviting. A few light bulbs on chains swayed from the ceilings, but they were too high to help much.

The nurses wore crisp, white pinafores and tall white caps. Actually, they looked more like chefs. Even though they were busy in this understaffed hospital, they took time to smile shyly and answer questions.

As if on cue, Nadia said, "This is the doctor who will lead us today." With a big smile she added, "She is also a sister in the Lord." The doctor was excited because they had just received their first x-ray machine. With great pride, she showed it to us. Then the doctor led us up four flights of stairs where we were to visit children in the critical care unit. Looking around, I saw that most of the children had strips of white bandages wrapped around their heads. Few of them moved. Yet their pain-filled eyes followed our every step. I had never felt so helpless.

But then Boris appeared. Bright orange and yellow, Boris

was my sock puppet of few Russian words; 17 to be exact. He didn't hesitate to say, "How are you? What is your name and Jesus loves you." His message was simple.

Word traveled quickly that a "thing on a hand" was talking. Curious medical and custodial staff crowded the hallways. Many had never seen a hand puppet before. Boris shook hands, tweaked noses, and kissed cheeks. "*Yey soos a blue was*" (Jesus loves you), he said over and over again.

"Barbara, a little girl is crying over there," Nadia said. "Go to her quickly."

Soon Boris was at the girl's bedside and in Russian asked her. "What is your name?"

With wide eyes and a surprised look, she said, "*Na ta sha.*"

Boris leaned over, kissed her nose and said, "Jesus loves you." Natasha giggled and reached over to pat my hand. Oh, I mean Boris' head.

Members of the team soon began handing out candy and stickers. Seeing an opportunity for fun, Boris perked up, babbled puppet words, and put stickers all over my face.

Now everyone was giggling and wanted a sticker, even the doctors and nurses. Bois kept up his act, but I cried on the inside. In America we take simple things for granted. In Russia, even a sticker became a treasure.

I left the hospital a changed person. The message of God's love was never meant to be complicated. A touch, a smile and even a puppet giving out stickers in Jesus' name are ways to live out the Gospel message.

Nadia and I ministered together translating the church services. I looked up Bible passages for her in English, and she would translate them into Russian.

"I want to be exact," she said.

Nadia took care of me while I was in Russia. Once, the group was going shopping, and somehow the bus left without me. Nadia missed me and instructed the bus driver to go back and get me because she knew I had planned to go.

It was not unusual for her to direct me to Russian people with whom I could share the Gospel. Another time, while visiting the prison, the warden asked us questions as to why we were there. No one spoke. Nadia nodded to me. I knew this was my clue to give him answers. "You may have one hour," he said. Please return to me after the hour and give a report.

I remember the day well. It was blustery, cold, and snowing. The ladies to whom we spoke were hungry physically as well as spiritually. Their faces were painted with color, but underneath their glitz showed a sad and forlorn emptiness.

In the short hour that we were given to speak, we shared about God's deep love and His forgiveness. Slowly, light reflected in distant eyes. God was moving among us. In that guarded prison cubical, 28 women raised their hands acknowledging their desire to receive Christ into their lives. The atmosphere in the room changed from hostility and anger to one experiencing the sweet, sweet presence of the Lord.

After an hour with the prisoners, we returned to the warden's office. His first question was, "How did you find my prison?" No one answered. Again Nadia looked at me. I stepped forward.

"Sir, the ladies said you treat them kindly and you are a fair man." He nodded. "They also said you give them more food than the other warden and they are grateful." He nodded again, taking my comments seriously.

As we left the prison that day in 1993, the guard who had been with us the whole time escorted us back to the bus. He climbed on and silently looked around. With deep emotion he said, "We have not heard such things before, and I can tell you our prison will never be the same again." With tears running down his face, he hurriedly left the bus.

His statement had a profound effect on me. I've not known Russians to weep easily. It took a lot of courage for the guard to tell us this. I remember that moment, the icy prison yard, the dingy walls, his worn uniform, the despair on the faces of the prisoners, the emptiness in the guard's eyes when we first met him. However, I also remember his tears and the light in his eyes when he left us. God made a difference in this man's life and we were privileged to experience it. He was correct; the prison would never be the same. God touched lives that day.

During the two weeks I was in Russia, Nadia and I sat together on the buses and talked about scriptural principles. We walked the streets and talked about the way Jesus lived. We talked about communism, Christian persecutions, forgiveness, sin, joy, righteousness, things God hates and things God loves. She had many questions and a thirst and hunger to know more about her living God. We prayed often and even sang together. It was a blessed time of Christian fellowship. I guess you could say it was a crash course in discipling or mentoring.

It was also the beginning of a long-lasting friendship.

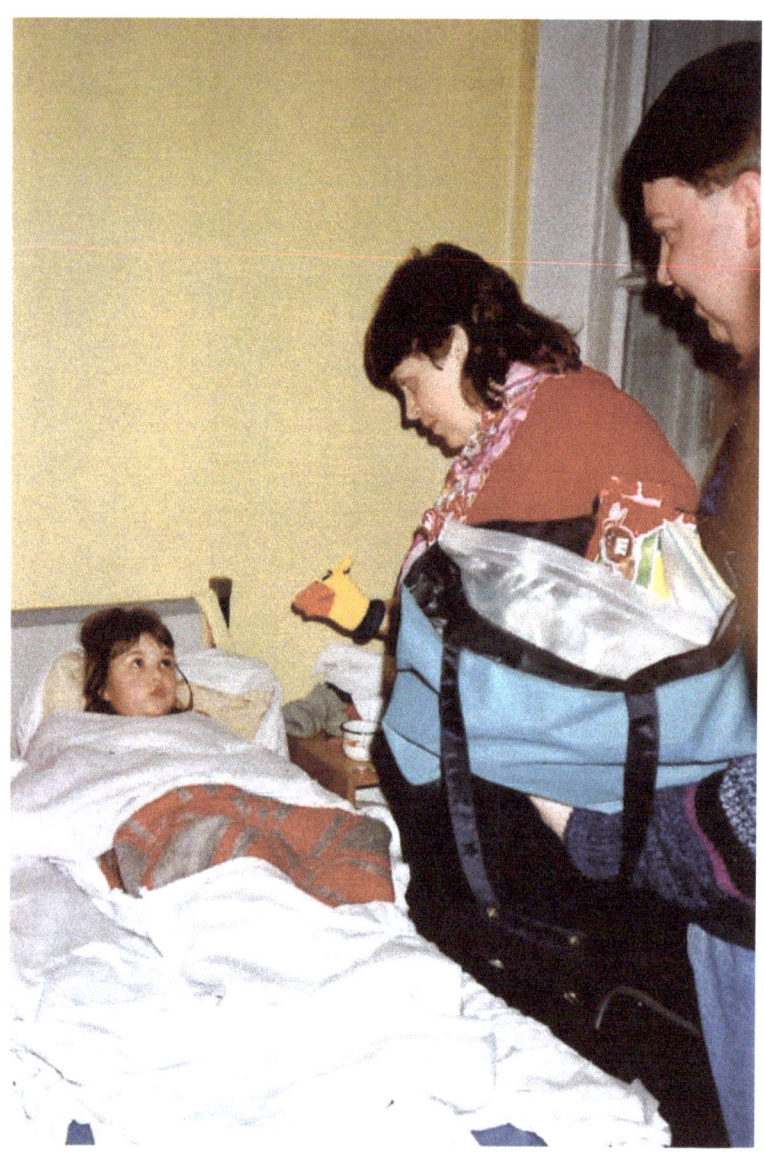

Visiting the hospital with Boris, my orange and yellow hand puppet

Hugs, Giggles, and Kisses

Russia, 1993

Slapping my arms against my sides for warmth and kicking the snow off my boots, I stomped down the stairs to the kitchen in the cellar of the Temple of the Gospel church. For 70 years prior to 1989, this church in St. Petersburg, Russia, had been used to house a metal factory. Now, the cheery kitchen and dining area served as a fellowship nook for weary Christians helping with the various ministries of the church.

The best part of going to the kitchen was being greeted by the babushka ladies (grandmothers, often called sisters) who worked there. These women, named for the scarves they wore on their heads, had weathered a lifetime of Communist rule. Despite it all, they continued to hold on to their strong Christian faith.

At times we couldn't communicate well because of the language barrier, but it didn't matter. God's joy was deeply etched in their faces, and their godly actions spoke volumes to me about their commitment to Christ.

During my two weeks in Russia, these sisters repeatedly ran up to me, said, "*Ya-low blue vaas,*" (I love you), gave me a big hug, giggled, and kissed me on the cheek. Giggling again, they would point upward to indicate God's love and run back to the kitchen.

In order to prepare our breakfast, the sisters often had to leave their homes at 4 A.M. and travel for two or three hours by foot and train in the bitter cold. Yet, they arrived happy and eager to serve us. We always had hot tea and bread. Sometimes we had kasha, a hot barley breakfast. Breakfast and most of our meals depended on what was available at the market.

The sisters let me help serve the meals to our team each day. It was hard work, but rewarding because we giggled, sang, and hugged a lot. I knew I had been accepted when they scurried toward me one day, tied an apron on me, and plopped a scarf on my head. They giggled and said, "Bab-ra see-ster now." Their love for me was genuine. I believe their depth of sensitivity and compassion was because God kept them close to His heart during the Communist reign.

One memory I'll always cherish is our group-singing times before each meal.

Sergei Nikolaev, the pastor at Temple of the Gospel, would say, "Let us all, Russians and Americans, brothers and sisters, stand, join hands, and sing praises to Almighty God together."

Before we had taken a breath, Sergei plunged into a hearty rendition of *What a Friend We Have in Jesus.* Hearing the familiar melody, the sisters would hurry from the kitchen, grab our hands, and with fervor, join us singing praises to the Lord.

It was a very emotional experience for me, this oneness. I cried most of the time I was in Russia. It appeared to me that the Russians glowed in their faith and were starved for unrestricted Christian fellowship. Through them, I learned the physical cost of sacrifice to do what Jesus would do. I watched them demonstrate unconditional love and kindness toward me and others no matter how inconvenient it was for them. They served the Lord with gladness and genuine hospitality. The Americans, on the other hand, were often haughty and took their faith lightly. I wondered at times who the real missionaries were.

With kitchen ladies,
"see-sters" from Temple of the Gospel

A Night to Remember

Russia, 1993

"Dear people," Pastor Nicolief stood up. "I have wonderful news for you." With tears in his eyes, he looked over his congregation. Everyone leaned forward as he paused and took a deep breath. "Our Irish brothers and sisters have driven over six days to come to us. And with them, they have brought 2,000 frozen chickens. Tonight, each family will get two chickens for their Christmas dinner."

Silence. Then thunderous applause and loud outbursts of sobbing echoed throughout the church. People shouted, "*Slava Boga*" (praise God). God has provided. It had been a brutal and lean winter. Most of the members from Temple of the Gospel church had bare cupboards and difficulty finding food. Two chickens would provide several meals for a family, and the stock would make delicious soup to warm them at night. Yes, God was good.

Our team clapped and shouted, "Praise God" along with the congregation.

It was priceless for me to witness the change in our brothers' and sisters' eyes as they transformed from despair to hope. All because of two chickens. It was probably the first meat they'd had all winter.

As American visitors, we had been invited to several Russian Orthodox Christmas Eve services. We hated to leave this joyful moment, but needed to hurry out to our waiting bus and attend the next service. The second service lasted nearly two hours. As soon as it was over, our leaders hurried us onto our bus to return us to our host church. There, we had a light meal before leaving to attend our third two-hour service.

When that service ended, the hour was getting late. So, with quick goodbyes, we thanked the people and hastened to our bus to head to the train station for our overnight trip to Moscow.

We were cutting the time close, so our driver dropped us off as near to the station as he could. The station was dark, but we could see the steam rising from the tracks as the hot train engine dripped slush. It was now 10:26 P.M. The train for Moscow was leaving in less than 15 minutes, and we weren't on it.

Hundreds of people pushed and shoved, almost stampeded, through the noisy train station. We took deep breaths, slung our bags over our shoulders and ran the last hundred yards to get to the train. Being forced back by the mob going the opposite direction was terrifying. I clung to Nadia's coat as tightly as I could as she plunged through the crowd.

"Don't let go!" Nadia screamed over her shoulder.

My fingers were slipping. The people were relentless in their shoving. If I lost my grip on Nadia, the train—and the only people I knew in Russia—would leave without me.

"Hold tight," Nadia yelled again.

Help, God. Please help me.

One unified thought seemed to exist for the masses: Get on that train. Now!

I was exhausted, my bag was heavy, and my feet were frozen, but miraculously God got us through the mob.

Oh, thank you, thank you, God. Thank you.

With minutes left before departure, we squeezed into the crowded train to discover only one sleeping compartment was left. Since Nadia and I and two seminary students, Dewey and Scott, were last to board, we had to share the compartment. We looked at one another as our eyebrows lifted in surprise. "Uh oh, now what?" As American Christians we'd assumed we would have separate compartments, one for males and another for females.

Observing the situation and our discomfort, Nadia said, "We must have four to a room, and it is okay. We are in Russia, and this is the way it is. Men take the top berths. Barbara and I will take the lower ones."

The compartment was clean, but old and worn. We had four berths, a side table, and a window. The hard berths weren't very wide, maybe two feet, but definitely not three. However, the beds did have clean white sheets on them. That was nice, although it was difficult to get comfortable on the thin mattress, and it was unbearably hot in the room. We were exhausted and went to sleep quickly.

Sometime during the night, the train began to jerk and slowed to a stop. How strange, I thought, since it was a non-stop train to Moscow. I cracked open my window to look outside, and also took a gulp of the brisk air. It was refreshing after the sweltering heat of the last several hours. It was then I saw the four-foot snow drifts and jagged barbed wire for as far as I could see.

Oh, my goodness. We're being taken to Siberia or a concentration camp! My heart, as well as my imagination, raced as I waited for guards with rifles to burst through our door, grab us, and leave us at a desolate camp. After about 10 minutes, the hissing of the engine revved up and the train began chugging along. I held my breath. *Is the door going to open now?* The minutes ticked by, but I heard no footsteps, and no one entered. The only sound came from the wind whooshing through the window. I plopped back down on the mattress. My heart calmed and my fears were laid to rest as I realized our stop had been to allow another train to pass.

At 5 a.m. I heard a rustling sound above. Then there was a thump in the room. We had been told that riders often got robbed on the train to Moscow. Was this one of those times? The door squeaked open, and as the light shone in, I saw Dewey exit.

After 25 minutes, Dewey returned. I was sitting up on my berth and I needed the restroom, but didn't want to leave until he came back.

"I ran into one of the conductors in the hallway," he said. "He was staggering drunk."

"I need the restroom, Dewey. What should I do?"

"It's not safe out there for a woman alone," Dewey responded. "I'll walk you to the restroom and walk back with you."

About 30 minutes after we returned from the restroom, our compartment door squeaked open. A conductor poked his head in and yelled a hearty "*Dobroye utro.* (Good morning) Time to get up." He walked to the table between the berths and put down a thermos of hot tea and four small glasses. I don't remember ever using a tea cup while in Russia. It always was a small glass, and hard to hold because it was hot.

Luba, our spunky Moscow guide, took us to the Kremlin and Red Square. Wow, the brilliant colors on the building and onion-shaped domes were magnificent. It kind of reminded me of being a princess in a castle in some kind of fairy land. While at the square, we had the joy of walking by a state wedding. It was snowing and the radiant bride had her new husband's overcoat thrown over her shoulders. She looked cold, but beautiful and happy. We waved and hollered, "Congratulations." She nodded, smiled, and even allowed us to take photos. In Russia, couples may have a traditional wedding ceremony, but they must also have a civil ceremony at the Department of Public Services. It is during this civil ceremony that rings are exchanged and the couple is pronounced husband and wife.

After the wedding, Luba took us to a 5-star hotel for a bathroom break. We looked scuzzy and very much out of place in our wrinkled clothes. Luba said, "The price for the elaborate hotel is $600 per night." During one of our conversations, Nadia had told me her salary was $10 a week. A citizen would need to work 60 weeks to pay for one night of this elegance.

Next, Luba took us to an elite café for a pre-ordered lunch. The only food I remember eating was cow tongue. It tasted like roast beef, although a little grainy. I enjoyed the experience of a new food, but once I found out it was tongue, my appetite waned a bit. Trying not to make a face, I ate it anyway to be polite.

We continued our sightseeing. Luba took us past the Russian White House. It didn't look like a house at all. To me it looked like a massive, rectangular apartment building or a place for business offices.

The group asked if there was a McDonald's. Luba told us the

only McDonald's in Russia was in Moscow. Opened in January 1990, it seated 900 people and had 25 cashiers. By this time our group was extremely hungry because they wouldn't eat the tongue served at lunch. They begged to go to McDonald's for a meal. "We can go for supper," Luba said, "But only if you all eat the same thing." We agreed.

She arranged for a representative to stand in line to order our food. When we arrived at 4:30 P.M., the representative had already been in line for 2 ½ hours.

"Do you think there are 500 people in line?" I asked Luba.

She didn't hesitate. "Oh, no, more like 1,000."

It was an incredible sight.

"Everyone is getting Big Macs, fries, and a Coke," she said.

The team cheered. Since we all had the same orders, the McDonald's workers carried our food to our bus. It arrived at 5:40, but we had a problem. We had to be at a final Christmas service by 6:00. Sadly, the team argued whether to stay and eat or attend the service. It got to the point we had to vote on it, and it was decided to eat along the way.

We arrived at the packed Christmas-night service late. We stomped in and up to the balcony, disrupting everything. Many of the elderly people sacrificed their seats and stood by the wall so the American guests could be seated. The team chatted and fidgeted about, not paying a bit of attention. It was rude and embarrassing. We stayed an hour and then received nudges from some of the leaders. A professor whispered, "It's time to leave to catch our train back to St. Petersburg." *Oh my!* We disrupted the service again with our banging and clunking around. Members of our team talked as we exited. There was no regard for the holiness of this service. Shame washed all over me at their behavior.

We made it to the station and boarded the train without the difficulties of the previous trip. I was relieved to have the same roommates as before—Nadia, Scott and Dewey. After settling in our sleeping compartment, it wasn't long before there was a knock at the door. Sasha, a Russian Christian traveling with us, hesitated, but he asked, "Could I come in to visit? All my roommates are sleeping and I feel so alone."

"Yes, please come in," Dewey said.

We anticipated Christian fellowship and the opportunity to know Sasha better. It sounded like a fun time ahead. Sasha gave us a relieved smile. Sure, we were crammed into the stuffy compartment. The berths were close overhead and sitting upright was uncomfortable, but we managed.

Sasha had lots of questions. He struggled with English, but the urgency to ask his questions was greater than the language barrier. He plunged right in and asked, "Who is God? How is it that He can love us? Wasn't He sad to have His Son murdered? Why should He forgive us? What is church like in America? Do Christians have Bibles, and how do you know when God speaks?"

These had been forbidden topics only a few years earlier. Sasha and Nadia told us about the time they were in the Communist Youth League. However, they were starved for knowledge and wanted to get back asking more questions about basic Christianity, not talk about Communism.

Sasha's most surprising question was, "How do you have fellowship in America as a Christian?"

Dewey scratched his beard and replied, "We have church socials with food, soft drinks, and maybe play games."

Then I said, "We visit together in homes for coffee, dessert, or a meal."

Both Nadia and Sasha gasped.

"You go to one another's homes?" Nadia shook her head and her mouth rounded into a huge oh! "This is hard to imagine. Always before, we had to get permission from the government to visit in homes as Christians." In 1993 their newfound freedom was still an adjustment for them.

The train jostled on and soon our discussion turned into a time of worship. In the seclusion of a cramped sleeping compartment, two Russian and three American Christians whispered songs of praise to Almighty God. Nadia had a raspy, but hearty voice. She started the song, "Sing Alleluia to the Lord." The rest of us joined in whispering the descant. It was beautiful, precious, holy, as if angels sang with us. They also wanted to sing "How Great Thou Art," "Amazing Grace," and "Silent Night." One by one, we reached across the floor to join hands. Then each of us prayed aloud in our native language.

Five days earlier, in different parts of the world, none of us had known the others existed. Now we were united in the family of God. Tears didn't drip; they streamed down our faces.

Wiping my eyes, I said. "Sasha, this is what we call fellowship in America. You can do this in your homes."

Sasha burst into fresh tears, grabbed his chest, and said in broken English, "This is my first time to experience such a thing. Yes, we can do this too. Hallelujah, I am so full, so happy!"

My heart was full, too.

Long after we hugged everyone goodnight and turned out the lights, I lay in my berth reflecting on this holy experience. My heart was broken. We had come to Russia as missionaries, but the Russians were the true missionaries to us. They had given us their best, their love, and showed many unselfish acts of kindness and sacrifice. They acted like Jesus toward us. Sadly, our team didn't reciprocate. I couldn't help but cry. I thought back on questions Sasha had asked. His eagerness and desperation to understand the Gospel message was clear. We had experienced religious freedom tonight. We were allowed to fellowship with other believers, and "how precious it [was] for brothers and sisters to dwell in unity." (Psalm 133:1 paraphrased)

Many of us in America have several Bibles. This is a freedom we in America take for granted, and a freedom people in Russia had yearned for and now dearly cherish.

My heart was overwhelmed with all that God has given us in a free country. Tears continued to spatter my bed.

Lord, forgive me for taking you and your gifts for granted. Please never let me forget this night. For surely it is a night to remember.

Sasha, the Christian brother who came to our compartment on the train

Tanya, God Loves You, Too

Russia, 1993

"Welcome to St. Petersburg. I am Tatiana, your tour guide." With a gleam in her eyes and a cocky smile she said, "*Yal-low blu-vas.* You will need to know this phrase for your stay in Russia. It means, 'I love you.' And now that I've told you 'I love you,' you may call me Tanya."

Cheers and applause roared throughout the bus. It seemed the Americans liked Tanya's spunk. Her grin broadened. This was her first time to host an American group, and she wanted to make a good impression. She knew she had become an instant hit with the American seminary students.

Tanya and I soon became friends. One morning while giving us a museum tour, she stopped in the middle of her talk and asked, "Barbara, how old are you? What does your faith consider wrong, and what do you think about virginity?"

The three questions startled me, but I answered them as best as I could. I realized I was talking with a Russian woman who had never heard of God, and had no concept of what a Christian was. Tanya needed to test me to see if she could trust me with deeper questions later on.

Two hours later, while browsing through a state-owned tourist shop, Tanya pulled me aside. "Barbara, my daughter is taking a German test now. Will you pray for her?"

I said yes, and told her I would go over to a corner of the shop to pray. She nodded and watched to see what I would do. After bowing my head and praying silently, I nodded to her that it was done. She nodded back and continued the tour.

Back at the hotel, I invited Tanya to my room for tea. She asked to use the phone to check with her daughter about the test.

With surprise she told me, "Olga got a perfect score!"

No sooner had we poured our tea than Tanya started asking questions. "Barbara, tell me more of your faith. Do you believe in the Old and New Testaments? What is the difference? How did you come to God? I have no concept of God. Who is God, anyway?

"Before our government changed everything, I believed in Communism and was an atheist. Now my beliefs are gone, and I don't know what I am. It is difficult, and I am lonely. Will you pray that I will find love, security, and happiness in my life?"

I agreed, but this time asked if I could pray with her right then.

"Yes, please do."

I put my arm around her and prayed for her. When we finished, I noticed tears in her eyes.

"You Americans are more flexible in your prayers than we Russians. You pray sitting, standing, and not always in a church. This is a new thing for me to comprehend."

I told her God would like to listen to her prayers, also. She nodded.

"It is later than I thought, Barbara," Tanya said grabbing her coat. "I must find bread for my family. Walk with me and I will show you how we shop in Russia."

Thrilled to be included, I tried to see everything all at once, but the ankle deep slush slowed me down. Tanya noticed and grinned. "We will do this the Russian way." She firmly linked my arm through hers, and we tromped down the street.

While Tanya and I walked, my mind kept reviewing the last two hours. Tanya needed to see if the Christian life was any different than hers. Going to the shops with her for bread was one more way for me to show God's love.

Shopping in Russia was eye-opening. It was not a simple task. The stores had no signs, but Tanya knew exactly where to go. She led me down some cellar steps to a meat market, then through another door to look for sour cream. Nothing was packed or bottled. She used a plastic container from her bag.

At the bread shop, the wait took forever. We stood in one line to ask the price, in another to get a receipt, still another to pay, and then back to the first line to pick up the single loaf of bread.

In that moment I saw Tanya not as the eloquent and efficient tour guide, but as my tired and hungry friend. She, as thousands of other Russians, went from one shop to another, hoping there would be food to buy for the next meal.

Our last stop was a fruit market. The tiny apples and oranges in the bins were dirty and bruised. Tanya seemed embarrassed. Nevertheless, with dignity she asked, "Barbara, would you like some oranges to share with your friends tonight on the train to Moscow?'

"How much?" I asked.

"About 103 rubles, or 22 cents."

I reached for my purse to pay, but she held me back.

"No! The oranges are my gift to you. I wanted to buy you porcelain in honor of our friendship, but I don't have enough money."

Knowing her income was $10 per month, I wanted to cry out, "Please don't spend your money on me. Save it!" Instead I hugged her and whispered, "Tanya, this is a wonderful gift. And now, may I give half of my oranges to you? They can help make your dinner special tonight."

"Barbara, the oranges are to share with your friends."

"Aren't you my friend, Tanya?"

"Indeed I am." She straightened. "It would be a pleasure for me to accept them." Tears again came to her eyes. She looked at me for a long time. "My family will have a very nice dinner now."

I found gift-giving to be an important part of friendships in Russia. Because I had accepted Tanya's gift first, she was then free to accept mine without disgrace.

On our final day in Russia, Tanya met us at the airport to say good-bye. It had been a week since I had seen her. I was concerned because we hadn't finished our conversation at the hotel.

After the customary hugs and kisses, Tanya got right to the point. She asked me one last time, "Barbara, will you pray for me again?"

I nodded. She bowed her head and grabbed my hands. When I finished my prayer, she said, *"Ahh mehn."*

Then Tanya looked me right in the eye. "Barbara, do you believe in Jesus Christ?"

"I certainly do."

Again I explained about Jesus' death for sinners, His resurrection, and God's love for her. Moments before I was to leave, she touched my arm and very quietly and reverently said, "I think I believe in Jesus' Father, the Almighty, but I am so confused. Please pray for me when you return to America."

Now both of us were crying and it was time for me to board the plane. It was a difficult goodbye, because I felt that everything was unfinished. Before leaving the final exit of the airport, I turned back to wave. "Tanya, God be with you, my friend."

She nodded back and with great emotion said, "It is so. He is with me."

As I remember Tanya today, I still pray for her.

> *I am sure that God, who began the good work within you*
> *will continue his work until it is finally finished*
> *on that day when Christ Jesus comes back again.*
>
> Philippians 1:6 NLT

With Tanya outside my three-block-long hotel

*MOLDOVA
1996*

Who Is Luba?

Moldova, 1996

Luba lived in Moldova and spoke no English.

I was asked to meet this unknown woman at the airport and give her some money. I was told not to worry and that somehow Luba would find me. It was the only information I received. Let me tell you, God is the only one Who could have worked out that situation.

When someone is traveling to a foreign country where there is little income and great need, family members often send cash with a trusted person to give to their loved ones. In most of the former Soviet Republic countries, letters and packages are "opened and inspected" to check for questionable contents. Oftentimes items get "lost," and cash usually is removed first…by whomever. When it was discovered that I was going to Moldova, I was asked by a friend of a friend of a friend to be that trusted person. This unknown person gave me money that would equal a Moldovan's salary for 1½ years. I was apprehensive. This was a lot of money!

We landed at the airport in Moldova where people butted in

front of us in line, stepped on our feet, and aggressively elbowed through the crowds trying to get to customs. It was scary. I felt an even greater urgency to get this money to Luba, but who was Luba?

When we got outside it was a little less crowded. Suddenly a beautiful, but sad-looking woman was at my side. She said several things in Russian to me. I didn't understand any of it. She tried again. I wondered if this was Luba. But then, what if it was someone else asking for money? Suppose I turned over the envelope of money and this was not Luba? I asked around to see if anyone spoke English. Someone did. He spoke with the woman, and told me I was to give her the money. She frowned and didn't understand my hesitation. I, through the interpreter, asked her sister's name, where was I from, and if she knew my name. She got a 100% on the test, and I fearfully turned over the money. She burst into tears thanking me and started talking rapidly. The interpreter said Luba wanted to meet me again at the airport when I left Moldova, so she could send candy to her sister. She shoved a phone number into my hand, told me to call her, and was off.

Calling her was a real problem because I couldn't find a phone. The night before we were to leave her country, I found a phone, attempted a garbled message in Russian to her husband and prayed that I would see her at the airport at sunrise the next day.

At sunup the next morning the whole team was scouting for Luba. No Luba! I was sick with concern. Our plane was leaving in less than 10 minutes! Customs pushed us to the head of the line and ushered us right up to the exit that led to the airstrip. It was at that moment I saw Luba standing out on the airstrip carrying a very large parcel. "Oh God," I prayed. "There is no way I can get to her now. Please help me." As if she heard my prayer, Luba turned around and looked me right in the eye. I waved and motioned for her to come inside. I rushed over to the inspectors, and asked if I could go meet my friend. They didn't understand me and turned me over to someone who spoke English. This person really didn't speak enough English to understand me either. Both of them, however, indicated that there was absolutely no way possible for me to leave the security section to see her. It was an emphatic No!! My heart was broken. She was so close and yet so far.

We were getting ready to walk through the exit doors to the airstrip when suddenly there were all kinds of shouts, stomping, and the sound of running feet. The inspector thrust a package into my arms and waved me on. It contained everything Luba was sending to America! Praise God! Our whole team burst into a cheer! God precisely worked out the timing for this miracle. To this day, I am amazed at what happened! Our God truly *is* an awesome God. Hallelujah!

With Luba, who received the money from America

Sunflowers, Backpacks, and Noodles

Moldova, 1996

Cars and trucks whizzed by on the right and left sides of the road. Drivers honked without pause as their tailpipes rattled and hit the bumpy roads. Insane drivers even skidded around corners and ran over curbs. We were driving through the countryside, but it seemed more like a bursting metropolis. It appeared to me there were no driving rules at all. There were certainly no lanes, no street signs or traffic lights.

Eight of us were on this mission trip: four women, three teen girls and Brian, our 16-year-old token male. We had landed an hour earlier in Chisinau, Moldova, the small country nestled between Romania and Ukraine, and were on our way to the town of Bendery. Until this trip, none of our team members, including myself, had ever heard of Moldova.

Beep! Beep! Honk! Honk! Beep!

A small, banged-up car hovered close to our left side, accelerated, and almost ran our van off the road.

"Oh my!" I gasped.

Beep! Beep!

A dusty, black utility truck cut in front of us. Our driver jerked the van to the right. Flapping my arms like a pelican landing on a pond, I bounced to the other side of the van before grabbing the back of the driver's seat.

"Whoa, that was a close one," I said to a wide-eyed youth who sat behind me.

Another car screeched around us and almost hit a vegetable truck head on. "Look out!" I screamed and raised my left hip. I guess I thought my injuries might be less if only half of me was on the seat behind the driver.

Our driver wiped the sweat off his face and yelled something in Russian. He swerved back to the left and continued to drive at lightning speed as if nothing had happened.

"God, have mercy on us," I prayed.

I looked behind me and saw several of the kids with their heads bowed and lips moving. It appeared my prayer wasn't the only one.

In addition to the constant noise and swerving, it was suffocating inside the van. There was no air conditioning. The driver was sweating like a leaky faucet, and he kept all the windows rolled up.

"Would you roll down the windows?" A voice hollered from two seats back.

"Nyet," The driver replied. "Air will make you sick. Anyway, they are locked."

Nauseated, I leaned against the window. *I am going to be sick, if I don't get some fresh air soon!*

Despite the haphazard driving and my nausea, I delighted in the beauty surrounding me. This was a countryside bursting with life. The sky was Mediterranean Sea blue. Goats and sheep munched on tall grass alongside the roads and throughout the rolling hillsides. Older women wearing patterned headscarves sat or stood along fence posts and sold apricots, pears, or bouquets of wildflowers. Others just visited or gossiped. These ladies, or Babushkas as they were often called, smiled and waved to us as the van passed them on the road.

My thoughts were interrupted by a chorus of "oohs" and "ahhs" that came from the girls in the back of the van. It was so loud, the van driver let out a deep belly laugh.

"You like, yes?" He asked and beamed like a new papa handing out cigars at the hospital.

What did we see? Surrounding us were miles and miles of giant, yellow sunflowers. They looked almost human with their dark faces, yellow hair and green leaves waving to us like arms in the breeze. The sun was setting; rays of sunlight shimmered and bounced off the fields like rivers of pure gold. In my entire life, I have never seen anything so lovely and magnificent.

"Oh Mrs. Barbara! Have you ever seen so many sunflowers before?" Lauren, the blue-eyed teen with the long blonde hair whispered.

"Wow!" Brian said. "That was totally awesome."

The girls continued their exclamations and praise and, as if at the final curtain call at a Broadway play, burst into thunderous clapping as we passed the sunflowers.

Sitting up straighter, the driver gave us a silver-toothed smile. Eugene, one of the interpreters, translated his words, "I knew you would like it! I knew it!"

The driver looked at us in the rear view mirror, waved his fist in victory and said, "It's like paradise, *dah?*"

Vigorously, we nodded our heads in agreement.

Although not my first time in a Russian-speaking country, this was my first time in Moldova. I had expected to see drab buildings, busy subways, and colorful onion-shaped domes as I had seen in Moscow and St. Petersburg.

Moldova wasn't like that at all.

The town of Bendery was both quaint and charming. Many of the buildings were covered in patterned blue mosaic tiles. It reminded me of Wedgwood blue china. Sitting areas had sidewalks laid in circular mosaic patterns of red, blue, yellow, and green.

Then there was the other side to Bendery. Buildings needed painting. Doors were half-hanging on hinges. Streets were cracked and the potholes were like a child's muddy play area. Many buildings had broken windows or no windows at all.

There had been a horrific war six years earlier and much of the town was destroyed by the bombs. It was hard to believe that this weathered, run-down town had once been a city of luxury.

As if reading my mind and with a proud look on his face, the driver began to speak. Eugene once again translated.

"Bendery was not always this way. Before the war it was beautiful. There were parks with fountains, flowers, and trees. The war destroyed everything; there was nothing left. We work hard. We are strong. And we start to smile again. It will be beautiful soon."

Men, shirtless and tanned, stopped their hammering and turned to stare as our van drove by. I saw lumber stacked against buildings. Piles of wood shavings and tools were scattered across different sites. The driver waved his arm toward the buildings. He swallowed hard. "No one receives pay for their work." There was a fierce pride and love for this town, and I knew it would be beautiful once more.

The grueling ride from the airport to the church took about an hour. After many near accidents, I was relieved for it to end. The driver slowed down and pulled into a grassy field near a church. I took a deep breath. Hallelujah! Here in one piece.

Soon it was time to meet our host families. Everyone was nervous, but excited, too. I wondered what our home would be like and if the people would like us. Of course they would like us, I assured myself. We're nice people. I'm sure we will like them, too. Our new home will be an adventure, a cultural experience, I gulped and reminded myself.

Mashie, our female interpreter, along with a short man with dark brown hair, a bushy mustache, and twinkling brown eyes walked over to our group. He waved his hand at us and said in his limited English, "I am Venya." He pointed at four of us. "You four stay my house. Short name, Vinnie," he said proudly and thumped his chest. Then he frowned as he pointed to our bulging suitcases and said, "*Nyet.*" He shook his head and repeated, "*Nyet.*"

Our mouths flew open and we looked at one another asking a silent, "Why?"

He repeated himself and said, "All suitcases stay at church. Put something in backpacks each day. That is all."

I was not expecting this. I had packed so carefully. Now I had to sort through all those crafts, candies, and gifts in my suitcase and take out a nightgown, an outfit for tomorrow, and a few personal items. Right in front of everybody. This was embarrassing. But we did as we were told. *I sure hope no one pilfers my bag tonight.*

"Why can't we take our suitcases, Mrs. Barbara?" Lauren asked.

"I don't know, Sweetie. That's what Vinnie said."

Perhaps Vinnie saw the question in our eyes and heard the concern in Lauren's voice. His face softened a little and he gave us a half smile. "You will see," he said and pointed his finger at us. "You understand soon," he added as he motioned for us to get into his car.

After the same kind of heart-stopping ride we'd had from the airport, we arrived at Vinnie's apartment located in the center of town. There were lots of trees, and no streetlights. A slight moon was out, but instead of illuminating, it only seemed to enhance the shadows being cast by the worn-down office buildings surrounding us.

Vinnie parked the car in front of his apartment and pulled out our backpacks. We uncurled our cramped legs, and in dresses, tried to gracefully exit the car.

Galina, Vinnie's wife, smiled and waved to us as she waited on the porch. We walked up the three steps and smiled back at her. Then she leaned over to hug each of us and immediately hustled us through the porch door into utter darkness. Here she paused. With an infectious laugh she spoke in Russian and Mashie interpreted. "We live on the seventh floor and the elevator is broken. There are no lights in the stairwell either, so you won't be able to see going up. Come."

Vinnie gave a hearty laugh. "Now you know why no suitcases.

Seven flights," he pointed up. "No elevator!" He chuckled again.

Galina turned and started up the stairs. One by one we followed. We weren't the only ones on the stairs. Other tenants were going up and down. I groped around until I found an arm to hold on to. I whispered, "Who's this?"

"It's me," Jeanette replied.

We laughed, giggled, and tripped up most of the steps in the dark stairwell. Somewhere around the fifth floor, we groaned and puffed for air. Sweat ran down my back. My backpack pressed against my denim dress and stuck to me like a wet towel. I felt like a tired and dirty pack mule climbing a mountain ridge.

I heard groaning and rasping sounds behind me.

"Mrs. Barbara, can we rest a minute?" Lauren panted.

Between wheezing and gulping for air I said, "No we can't stop now, I can't see where Galina's going."

We trudged on and finally reached the seventh floor. Our legs shook and trembled like limp spaghetti. Sucking in air and blowing it out as fast as our racing hearts would allow, we stood still. Sweat dripped off our foreheads as we bent over to untie our sneakers. We lined them up against the wall, and with a deep breath, entered Galina's apartment.

I glanced around the small, dimly-lit room. Even though it was very dark, I noticed a red sofa against the back wall, a brown covered chair, and a wooden table. Hanging on the wall was the familiar scenic blanket so common in many households. I smiled. Shaking my head back and forth, I mumbled a quiet, "Oh yeah, so Russian."

Each window was draped in white European lace curtains. Floor length, too. That was quite a surprise. Nice touch.

The kitchen was small with room for only three people. Under the counter was a refrigerator just a little bigger than one in an American university dorm room. The pumpkin-orange cabinets were trimmed in white. Plants and vines were strung between the cabinet tops and the curtains. The homeness was warm and cozy. Galina really had a flair for decorating, and I decided this house was more colorful than the ones I had seen in Russia. Who knew that later in the week, Galina would teach us how to make borscht, often called red soup, in this inviting nook.

Galina took Jeanette and me down the hall to her and Vinnie's bedroom.

"Vinnie and I will sleep on the sofa in the living room. It's no problem." Then Galina left to take Mashie and Lauren to the guest room.

Our bed had a crisp, white duvet and two fluffy pillows. It looked good to me. I was exhausted. We had a small balcony about two feet away from the headboard. Galina had some clothes out there drying and a few potted flowers by the railing. She told us to leave the door open so we would get fresh air. With barely enough space to move in the room, we had to put our backpacks on top of one another. Despite its size, the room was clean and comfortable.

Jeanette saw me looking at a picture on the wall. "Is that who I think it is?" she asked.

"Yep, Joseph Stalin, the Communist leader. Weird, huh?"

"Yeah it is. Look at the way his eyes glare down at us. No matter where we go in the room, it's like he's watching us." Jeanette whispered. "It gives me the creeps."

"Me, too. Let's cover his face tonight when it's time to go

to bed."

"Sounds good to me," she said.

Galina took us to a room that held a bathtub and a sink, and showed us how to twist the knobs to get water for baths. The hot and cold faucets were on the opposite sides than in America. Then she told us we were too late to have hot water for our baths, because the government didn't allow hot water after 10 P.M. Next, she showed us the toilet room and the can in which to put used toilet paper. There was no sink in the room, so we would have to go back to the bathing room to wash our hands.

After taking ice cold baths and changing into clean clothes, we gathered back in the living room for an 11:30 P.M. supper of boiled potatoes, cucumbers, bread and the fruit drink called compote. We chatted with our hosts, and I tried to force my eyelids to remain open. After an hour, we said our good nights and headed off to our bedrooms.

At 3 A.M. I woke up and shook Jeanette. "I'm on fire! Something is stinging me all over, and it really burns."

"Me too," she whispered. "It's awful!"

Jeanette was thrashing on the bed and slapping her arms and face as fast as I was. "I think we're being eaten alive by mosquitoes," she said as she got up and dug around in her backpack. "Here, try some of this cream. It's supposed to stop itching."

I took the tube and slathered the cream on my face, arms and legs. "Ugh." It was thick and heavy, and it made me sticky and hotter than I already was.

At 3:45 A.M. there was a blood-curdling screech outside on the balcony. I sat straight up in the bed. My heart felt like it was beating faster than bullets being fired from a machine gun.

Jeanette bolted up, too.

"Did you hear that scream?" I asked. "What do you think it was?"

"I don't know!" Jeanette said as she grabbed my arm. "It was horrible. Do you think someone is being killed?"

Again we heard, *RArrrhhhhhhh! RArrrrhhhhhhhh!*

With a long sigh, Jeanette whispered, "I think it's a rooster."

"Are you kidding me? A rooster?" It sure didn't sound like a rooster to me. There was no English sounding cock-a-doodle-do anywhere in that rooster's squawk. "This bird's got it all wrong," I mumbled. "It's the middle of the night!"

"This is Moldova, Barbara. Maybe roosters wake up early here."

Convinced it was a rooster, I flopped back down on the bed and tried to go back to sleep.

RArrrhhhhhh! RArrrhhhhhh!

I cringed and whispered, "Dumb old bird."

He screeched every 20 minutes for the next three and a half hours.

Not rested at all, we rolled out of bed, got dressed, and had almost finished loading our backpacks when we heard another unusual sound. *Cluck, cluck, wock, wock, wock cluck!*

"What's that?" I stared at Jeanette.

Soon we heard flapping and a strange kind of sound like singing. I froze.

"Jeanette, *what* is going on?"

She giggled. "Look out on the balcony. That hen just laid an egg!"

"A hen? You're kidding. Up here on the seventh floor?"

"Uh, huh."

We tidied our room and joined the others for breakfast. As Galina smiled, her first question was, "Did the mosquitoes bite you?"

"Oh yeah," Jeanette said. We showed her our arms and legs.

"I will see if I can make it better for you tonight," She grinned and whispered like telling a secret, "They ate Vinnie and me, too."

"Galina, was that a rooster on the balcony?" I asked.

"Yes," she replied. "The neighbor on the right keeps his rooster on the balcony, and the neighbor on the left side has hens and chicks on hers." I shook my head.

Vinnie left us girls to get the car. The four of us got our backpacks and tromped down the seven flights of stairs. In contrast to the total blackness of the stairwell overnight, the sun now shone brightly through the open porch door, allowing us to see the steps. I made a mental note to remind the girls to bring their flashlights with them tonight.

I scrunched into the front of Vinnie's compact car. Mashie, Jeanette, and Lauren crowded into the back for another death-defying ride, like we'd had the day before. The drive to the church took around 20 minutes. We arrived at noon and lunch was ready. Members of the other team had arrived an hour earlier but waited on us.

Soup, bread, cucumbers, pancakes with cheese, compote, and hot tea were on the table. The kitchen ladies in their bright headscarves got us seated right away and stood beside the wall. The pastor motioned for us to stand for prayer. We did and afterward said our first *Ahh mehn* together.

Unfortunately, as I sat down, the pocket on my dress caught the edge of the soup bowl. The bowl flipped over and little round, homemade noodles flew up in the air, some of them puddling into my lap! Like a time warp, everyone paused with mouths open to see what I would do.

"Oh my goodness," I sputtered as my arms shot up like being held at gunpoint.

The cook sucked in her breath and covered her mouth with her hand! I could feel the heat rising on my face. I looked at the pastor then shook my head and laughed. What else could I do? There were noodles everywhere: on me, the table, the floor. Shoulders relaxed, eyes twinkled, and the kids slapped their thighs with laughter. The interpreters wiped tears from their eyes, and the pastor bowed his head and held his fist over his mouth.

"Oh, I'm so sorry," I said, trying to sound dignified and remorseful. "I'm okay." But then I pictured all those curly noodles flying through the air and I started giggling again. I glanced over at one of the kitchen ladies as she turned her back, her shoulders rising up and down.

Assured I had not been burned, the kitchen ladies went into mother mode. With efficiency and Cheshire-cat grins, they scattered about. One lady scooped noodles from the puddle on my dress. Another one wiped up the broth under my feet and on the table. The third comforted me and patted my shoulder over and over. The fourth one hurried back to the kitchen to get me another bowl of hot soup.

"*Spasiba bolshoy,*" I said, attempting my first "thank you very much" in Russian. The kitchen ladies' faces lit up, and they swarmed back to me like bees going to honey. I was swooped into arms, and given a hug and a kiss on the cheek by each lady.

My inconvenient accident gave us an opportunity to laugh and relax together. Perhaps being covered in noodles and being tended to by so many caring people wasn't a bad way to conclude the first 24 hours in Moldova. The people were kind and gracious, and I liked them immediately. I smiled and wondered what the next 24 hours would bring.

Vinnie and Galina's apartment was on the 7th floor, wtih no elevator!

Vinnie, with Galina in the background, getting ready to take us back to the church. We stayed with them several nights.

Galina in her cheery orange kitchen

Am I Being Kidnapped?

Moldova, 1996

I WAS HOME ALONE behind a high, locked security gate when I suddenly heard a scraping sound nearby. My eyes flew open and I was startled to see an unknown man standing at my bedroom door. He said something and frantically motioned for me to get up and go with him. *Oh my goodness! Who is this man? What does he want and what is he saying?*

Two days earlier our team had moved from the town of Bendery to Tiraspol. Four of us girls were staying with Rasita, a widow, and her older children, Zhanna and Igor.

The man at the door cleared his throat, said something else, and motioned again for me to follow him. Igor now stood beside him, and he didn't seem worried. He nodded for me to go with the man. I had a three-inch blister on the bottom of my foot from the long walk around Tiraspol the day before. Trusting Igor, I carefully pulled a shoe onto my painfully swollen foot, then limped to the car to go with the stranger.

He didn't talk to me, except to say, "Twenty-five kilometers" (about 15 miles). After 20 minutes of driving I wondered, *Am I being kidnapped?* Twenty-five, 30, 35 minutes passed. *Oh Lord. What's going on? This is strange.* I was getting nervous. About that time, the man swerved the car to the right and stopped near a grape arbor in the middle of nowhere.

Then I saw them! There stood my team members! Hallelujah! What a sight! *Thank you, Jesus! I haven't been kidnapped!* I couldn't wait to get out of the car and hug their necks.

Since I had stayed at home to rest my foot, I didn't know about the change of plans. After day camp, our team had been invited at the last minute, to do a Bible Club and lead the worship service for a village church in another district. My surprise "kidnapping" was to assure me I had not been forgotten when the plans changed.

This new church held its services under a grape arbor. Rickety, hand-made wooden benches served as our "church pews." Rich, luscious grapes hung over us on horizontal poles. Patches of a sapphire-blue sky and green branches colored our "ceiling." We even had a breeze! It was beautiful. It was peaceful. It was needed.

Our youth team did a tremendous job of teaching. Using puppets, they presented the story of Noah, then led the children in singing. They also shared testimonies and taught crafts using crosses and yarn. I was proud of them.

After three hours of interacting with the grape-arbor children, we were given the surprise of our lives. The members of that congregation led us around to the other side of the arbor where we saw a partially-completed church building. But that wasn't all. Once inside, we carefully walked on planks, around buckets and over tools. We hugged the rough, cement wall as they led us down makeshift steps into a basement type of area. At the bottom, our gasps of delight brought smiles to the faces of the people standing along the walls. There—in the middle of a muddy, half-finished room—was a banquet feast! It was beautiful.

There were no lights, only the soft hue of candlelight on the linen-covered tables where 30 place settings were arranged with mixed pieces of china.

The meal consisted of platters filled with apricots, cherries, plums, breaded vegetables, tomatoes, cucumbers, tarts, bread and butter, and the ever-present pots of tea. We even had thermoses of freshly-squeezed milk! I have no idea how they prepared the meal. There were no cars, houses, kitchens, or cows near us. Each of us recognized the sacrifice, generosity, and labor in such a loving gift. It was a very emotional and humbling experience.

When we thought we had been "blessed to pieces," they blessed us more. While we sat around the table laughing and talking with the congregation, one of the women started playing her accordion. All of the Moldovans burst into a melodious hymn of praise to God. Then they sang *Amazing Grace* in Russian. We were overcome by this outpouring of love; all we could do was cry. Then we tried to laugh. Then we had to cry some more. The feast, the music, and the fellowship was like a treasure chest of love; a priceless gift I will value in my heart for the rest of my life.

How good and pleasant it is, when brothers live together in unity (Psalm 133:1).

Ephesians 5:19-20 is what I saw that day: *Speak to one another with psalms, hymns and spiritual songs. Sing and make music in your heart to the Lord, always giving thanks to God the Father for everything, in the name of our Lord Jesus Christ* (NIV).

Children making string crosses under the grape arbor

Americans and Moldavians singing along
with the woman playing the accordian after the banquet

The surprise banquet in the half-finished basement
on the other side of the grape arbor

Birthday Party at Masha's & Whisked Off to Prison

Moldova, 1996

Masha, one of the cooks at the church in Tiraspol, invited us to her apartment on Saturday to celebrate the fifth birthday of her son, Igor. The mission team was excited about another new adventure and couldn't wait to get back to our suitcases to see what kind of children's gifts we could dig out!

Saturday came. We squished into the van laughing, singing and wondering what a Moldovan birthday party would be like. To our surprise, the party first consisted of a breakfast of blini (Russian pancakes), pastries, cake, and of course, hot tea. The next part of the party was to walk about two miles to the forest and the Dniester River. No one had bathing suits, but that didn't stop Brian, our one male. He plunged into the river and had a blast. The rest of us watched longingly.

After the trip to the river, Masha took us back to her home for the birthday lunch. The tiny, three-room apartment was scorching hot from the many hours of baking. Nevertheless, she continued to prepare a tasty feast of soup, meats, vegetables, and salads. Igor wasn't paying much attention to his birthday lunch; he was more interested in the presents on the side table! I wonder why?

After eating, we sang "Happy Birthday" in English, and the next thing we knew, we were hurriedly being pulled out the door. We were informed that we were doing a church service at the women's prison…and were already late. *Oh, my!*

When we got to the prison, we discovered that they were not expecting us. The guards were quite distressed, but after much negotiation, they allowed us to have the service. God was totally in control because we were not prepared for this. We started out with singing. *Lots* of singing. That helped all of us loosen up, and we were able to joke around and laugh with the prisoners. Several kids shared testimonies. I sang a solo. Others read scriptures.

One young prisoner sitting on the back row elbowed inmates and with a stern, "Be quiet," "Shhhh," and "Move over," she aggressively maneuvered herself from the back row to the middle row. Then she continued her forceful pattern until she was right in front of us. She leaned forward to hear every word. At the end of the service, she asked question upon question. She was eager to know more about God. She was surprised when Jeanette told her that God loved her…and even more surprised to know that God wanted to talk to her.

At a pause in the conversation, Jeanette looked up and whispered, "What do I do now?" Almost in unison the team chorused, "Share the wordless book!"

A condensed version of the wordless book follows:

- The black page stands for sin. The Bible teaches that all have sinned and fall short of God's perfect standard.
- The red page stands for the blood of Jesus, which was shed for our salvation.
- The white page stands for the cleansing of salvation. Once we accept Christ, we become a new creation.
- The gold page stands for heaven. Jesus has gone to prepare a wonderful place for those who choose to accept Him.
- The final page, the green page, stands for growth. The Christian needs to grow in His new life.

Jeanette shared the book and asked the young woman, Lola, if she wanted to pray. Lola barely let Jeanette finish before she said, "I want to pray, too. How do I become a Christian?" Jeanette led Lola in a prayer of repentance. With hardly a breath after the amen, Lola's eyes flew open and she started smiling and clapping her hands in joy. "Oh it is wonderful! He's in me! I feel Him! I feel God!"

I had never seen such a quick transformation. The peace and joy that radiated from Lola was, without a doubt, the presence of the Lord. When the living Lord comes to dwell in a person, it is something that cannot be faked. We *all* knew we had experienced a miracle. It was a precious and blessed moment.

What a birthday celebration it was! We celebrated Igor's physical birthday and we celebrated Lola's spiritual birth-day. We left the prison singing and crying with joy. Christian inmates followed us to the gates. They, too, sang as they linked their arms through Lola's. Prisoners and team members alike wept together as we parted. Our lifestyles were different, but because of God's grace and forgiveness we were all one family in Christ.

We experienced the truth that day in prison.

NOTE: The Wordless Book was designed first by Charles Spurgeon in 1866. It still is being used today and can be ordered through Child Evangelism Fellowship (CEF).

Masha and her husband with Birthday Boy, Igor, and other children

God Interpreted for Us

Moldova, 1996

Through Mashie, our interpreter, I learned that Rasita used to walk 2½ hours each way to work. Because she did this for years, she developed varicose veins in her legs and had to have surgery. Not wanting her children to know about the surgery and worry, as soon as the doctor left the recovery room, she slipped out of the hospital and walked home. As a result, her stitches split open and she nearly bled to death.

One of Rasita's three jobs was likened to social work. Daily, she visited elderly people and walked miles attempting to purchase bread for these individuals. Oftentimes, she stood in lines for hours, only to be told all the bread had been sold. During one visit the previous year, she had gone outside to discover her bicycle had been stolen. Although she tried to be brave, she cried all the way home because there was so much to carry and a long distance to walk.

Rasita's story is not all sadness. There are encouraging things to tell as well. The language barrier made communication a definite challenge. But perseverance made it a splendid treasure.

Yes, I read and spoke some Russian. But it was not enough. One of the main ways Rasita tried to talk to me was through the message in her eyes. At times, it seemed as if her eyes bored a hole into my soul as she desperately tried to communicate her heart to me. Have you any idea the frustrations we both felt as she tried to share with me her fears, hopes, joys, disappointments, love, trust, tiredness, and concern for her family? Neither of us could speak the other's language. Yet, the eyes, the heart, and the actions spoke volumes. It was a gift in silence.

There was a day when I didn't have Mashie to interpret, so Rasita and I had to communicate totally on our own. It was the most cherished day of all, because God did the interpreting for both of us. We sat on stools under a cherry tree while baby ducks and chicks scurried over our feet. Rasita pulled out a well-worn Russian hymnal and pointed to a song. Then she started singing in a raspy, broken voice. I joined in. She pointed to the words and I stumbled through them. With fervor, we sang for 45 minutes. To this day, I have no idea what I sang, but my heart knew they were praises to God.

After singing, I tried to tell Rasita I wanted to pray for her. Somehow, she understood and grabbed my hand, leading us back to my bedroom. Here we dropped to our knees. I opened my mouth to pray in English, and it came out in fluent Russian. Sobbing, Rasita grabbed me and exclaimed over and over again, "*Ya pa ni mi ya! Ya pa ni mi ya!*" which means, "I understand! I understand." That was God at work, because I didn't know that much Russian! God knew she needed to hear and understand that prayer. He also knew we both needed to know it was His power that did it. Rasita then prayed, earnestly pouring out her heart to God. I never did understand what she prayed, but God did. She was a different woman afterward. A quiet joy and peace radiated from her.

God met with us and spoke to our hearts that day. He crossed our language barrier and increased our faith. God's promise in Jeremiah 29:12-13 (NIV) tells us, *Then you will call upon me and come and pray to me, and I will listen to you. You will seek me and find me when you seek me with all your heart.* Through the language of hearts seeking Him, God showed us that the presence of the LORD was surely in that place.

Meeting the Deaf Believers

Moldova, 1996

AS SOON AS WE FINISHED the service at the church, the pastor ushered our group out the door and into vans to take us to another church service. We sped along the dusty roads and screeched to a halt. The church service had already started. We were sooooo late. Next, we discovered we were supposed to be leading the entire service. *Talk about stress!* The pastor asked Eugene, our dear, 19-year-old interpreter, to preach a sermon and told the rest of us to provide special music and share four testimonies. I pointed to four in the group as we made our way to the front. Then, we sang *Po-Alleluia-Gos-pa-do* ("Sing Alleluia to the Lord"), our one and only Russian song.

While singing, I looked out at the congregation and noticed a group of deaf people. My heart leapt within me. I turned toward them and started signing the song we sang. Their faces lit up like a brightly decorated Christmas tree! We had connected. What a moment it was for me!

After the service all the deaf people gathered around me. We were a tangle of arms, necks and tears as everyone wanted to give and receive a customary hug and kiss. Through their interpreter, who talked to my interpreter, they bombarded me with questions. "What is your name? What is the American sign for sing? Are there deaf people in America, too? Will deaf people come to visit us in Moldova? How do you know sign language? Will you come back?"

They were starved for attention and Christian fellowship and showered me with love. I could hardly get through the experience without breaking down and sobbing right there in the sanctuary.

Later that night, I wrote in my journal: "Dear Jesus, This will probably be one of the highlights of my trip. It is evident these people truly love you. What a joy it was to meet them; I am so grateful. God, I promised them I would sign a song just for them on Sunday. I need you to help me find and memorize a song fast. Please let my hands glorify you, my beloved Jesus, and minister to these dear, dear people. Amen."

Our deaf friends were excited about our group coming back. As a surprise for them, I taught the Moldovan children a song in sign language. Sunday arrived and, sure enough, the deaf came back. In addition, they brought with them twice as many deaf friends! Oh my, it was exciting! English, Russian, English sign language and Russian sign language were all being spoken at one time.

Before I left the church that day, Ghemma, one of the deaf men, gave me a lovely oil painting of mountains and water. In fact, he handed it to me still wet. He told me this picture was a gift from the deaf brothers and sisters. It was a reminder of their love and gratitude to me for sharing Jesus with them. His final words to me were, "Who will come and teach us more about Jesus? Please don't forget us. When will you come back? Remember…we love you…."

Me (in the center wearing a blue headscarf),
with 16 deaf members at the church in Tiraspol

Saying Goodbye

Moldova, 1996

It was our last night at Rasita, Zhanna, and Igor's house. Zhanna had given me her bed for the week and was sleeping on a pile of mattresses in a corner of the hallway. Wanting to surprise her, I had hidden presents under the covers on her mattresses. When Zhanna laid down that night, the crinkling of the packages scared her and she tumbled off the mattresses and onto the floor.

Next, I heard squeals of delight and "*Var-var-rah!*" (Barbara!) She ran into my room and covered me with hugs and kisses. "Mama look," she said to Rasita as she held up one of the gifts. I had planned to hide Rasita's gift also, but it seemed more appropriate to give it to her then.

We chatted, more like gestured, without stopping. Finally, at one in the morning, we blew kisses good night. I was exhausted, and for the first time in two weeks, I immediately went to sleep.

In less than 10 minutes my door banged open, the light came on, and I was being roused from bed. Before I had my eyes open, Rasita and Zhanna were pulling a shirt down over my pj's.

Nodding yes, they pulled it back off. Then I felt another shirt being pulled over my head. Once again nods of confirmation. By now, I was waking up and wondering what in the world was going on. Then they gave me a sweater to try on. It also fit! They were excited and clapped. I clapped, too, although I still didn't know what was going on. Seeing my puzzled look, Zhanna hurried to get my dictionary. Pointing to the words, Zhanna told me they wanted to give me some of their clothes so that I wouldn't forget them. There was such joy in their eyes as they gave me these gifts. I burst into tears. Needless to say, I didn't sleep much the rest of the night.

I got up at 5:45 the next morning and walked through Rasita's garden. On my way back from the outhouse, the tears again started. I silently tried to say goodbye to this new world of friends that had opened their lives and hearts to me.

Rasita was watering the garden. She put down the hose and motioned for me to sit with her on the bench. We sat in silence while I continued to cry. Oh, the frustration of the language barrier! Most likely, Rasita, her family, and I would never visit with each other again. Both of us knew that in two hours my team would leave to finish our work in Bendery. I stood, then took a deep breath, gave her a hug and left to finish packing.

As I leaned over my suitcase, for the second time in six hours my door burst open. Here came Rasita bearing more gifts. She handed me her long Russian spoon used to stir fruit compote and her board used for cutting bread. Once again, these were gifts of personal value, so I "wouldn't forget" them. How could I forget such a dear family who unselfishly shared everything they had with me?

The pastor arrived soon after and drove us to the church for a farewell breakfast. Many of the beloved church members came to see us off. They served us a feast of apricots, potatoes, spaghetti soup, and pancakes. Zoya even played the accordion! We ate, laughed, and sang our praises to God. It was a glorious and holy time.

During our two weeks, we had been welcomed, hugged and kissed, and loved in this tiny church in Tiraspol. Without a doubt, we loved them back. Smiling children crowded around us and with outstretched arms hugged their goodbyes. Babushkas (grandmothers) kissed our cheeks. After the pastor prayed, the church members stood among us. They linked their arms through ours, and in Russian started singing *God Be With You 'Til We Meet Again*. For once, we didn't need interpreters because our hearts spoke for everyone. Church members, as well as our team, wept.

As transport cars began to arrive, we knew in minutes we'd leave this precious town and our wonderful new brothers and sisters in Christ. For me, the hardest part was when Zhanna and Rasita ran to the car and clung to me through the window as the car drove away. All three of us were sobbing and shouting over and over again, "*Yallow blue vas, Yallow blue vas*" (I love you, I love you). I held on to their arms, then hands, and finally their fingertips as long as I could.

My heart whispered to God, hoping the message would reach them: *God Be With You 'Til We Meet Again.* Then the car turned the corner....

Me in blue and Rasita in red

Letters from Transnistria, the Unrecognized State of Moldova

1996-1997

AFTER I RETURNED HOME from Moldova and in between trips, I received several letters from friends during 1996 and 1997. These are some excerpts from four of them.

Parts of Zhanna's last letter are sad; other parts are quite a blessing. This letter was six months in getting to me, and I was afraid we had lost contact. Once again, God got letters through! I am grateful for this. Please bear with the sentence structure and grammar. These excerpts are written exactly as they were translated for me. As you read them, please remember to pray for God's mercy and provisions for these dear brothers and sisters in a land so far away.

>Letter #1
>
>Hello Dear Barbara,
>
>We didn't get letter from you for a long time. Probably you didn't get mine. I got your map of the U.S.A. I dreamed

about this map for a long time. Now I will understand a little bit when somebody will speak about the United States, and I will have some sense about your place where do you live to compare with the whole globe.

In July, I passed the state exam and got the diploma of doctor [M.D.]. We have to practice as an intern for one year after the diploma. My salary is $10 a month. Right now, in October, the doctors finally got their salaries from July. For two months I was very depressed because I feel I killed my better years of life, my youth, to get my education, and now that I am working, it is only enough for pocket money. In addition, before, it was free for doctors to ride the public bus. Now it is $6.50 a month for a special bus pass, and I only have $3.50 left.

After internship, I will get special recognition and certificate and make a little more money. Then I will be preferable. And of course, God didn't leave me without his mercy. I have another job that pays two times more. It is like a maintenance job. After my medical job, I am running to the other end of the city to work as a street sweeper.

Barbara, understand me correctly, I am not asking for pity and I am not asking for help. I am very sad because I was born in this country, forgotten by God and because of that the city is damned by God. God will not send His mercy to this country because more and more days people are turning their faces away from Him. We have a law now, which prohibits religious meetings openly on the squares and streets. It is against Baptists.

Igor and his friend decided to evangelize the population by showing a movie about Jesus Christ. After a whole week of asking for permission to show this movie, they were only allowed to show it once and without conclusion or prayer afterwards. Then they decided to show the movie without permission. A deputy saw them and came by and drove his car over the wires and everything stopped.

We are alive and keeping. Dear Barbara, we remember you all the time.

I love you.

Zhanna.

Anna, petite and weathered looking, was in the women's work-release program in prison. During her stay in prison, she came to know the Lord. I saw in Anna a sweetness and a deep joy that can only come from knowing Jesus Christ personally. She knew she had done wrong, but also knew the prison was her mission field. Anna used every opportunity to tell her fellow inmates about the transformation and peace that her sweet Jesus had brought her. In her letter to me she wrote:

> Letter #2
>
> With best wishes to you. Your sister in God, Anna. To you, Var-Var-rah, our sister. The Christian sisters of the church, in our prison, want to send you best wishes. Come here one more time because all women liked you. You sang well and told encouraging stories. Please don't forget us. I will wait for your letter.

Masha, whom we lovingly called "Mashie," was our female interpreter. She was then in her third year at the university and had just turned 21.

> Letter #3
>
> As an interpreter, I was assigned to work for the photographer at the Festival of Jewish music and dance. The main purpose of this festival was to share Jesus with all

people. There were many people from the USA, Germany, Finland and Russia at the festivals. Many people repented and received Jesus. I attend church twice a week. I want to serve God with all my heart, He is the best friend in my life. I owe my life to Him….I love you, my sister and hope to hear from you, maybe we'll meet again. I'll be happy to see you and your husband in Moldova!

Finally, I would like to share with you some of Rasita's letter. Rasita, was a widow of 19 years, and was 54 years old at the time I met her. She lived with her daughter, Zhanna, a doctor, and Igor, her 18 year old son. Rasita wrote:

Letter #4

Peace to you and your house. I am rereading your letter and I am ashamed because I postponed my answer for a long time. Dear sister, I am from morning to night at my work. And at night I am barely able to crawl to my bed because I am so tired. You have seen what kind of life we have here. Our women are so tired.

I would like to be with you very much and speak to you by using our language which is understandable only by us. If God prolongs our lives until maybe next year, you will be back. It is more simple and easier for you to get to Moldova than us to get to you.

My son Igor was baptized in August.

Fall is very rainy and all summer was without any rain. We will have no harvest at all. Nothing grew up properly. From all the many things you saw in the pictures you took here and you sent to us, they are all now missing. Our neighbor's dog came to our yard and ate the chickens. Eight of our ducklings have passed away.

Thank you for prayers which you lifted up to God for

us. Thank you, Jesus, that we have some friends so far away from us and they are praying for our prosperity. Write everything about you. We miss you and will wait for your letters. I kiss you and please say hello to the brothers and sisters from our hearts. Love, Rasita.

I hope these letters give you a little more insight into how our fellow brothers and sisters in Christ have struggled in their lives and faith, yet survived.

NOTE: To better understand the conflict of Transnistria and Moldova and why Transnistria is called "the state that doesn't exist," please read about the Transnistria war from November 2, 1990-July 21, 1992.

Moldova
1998

Map of Moldova

The Second Was the First

Moldova, 1998

I'M SENDING YOU A PHONE NUMBER to use in an emergency. If you have to leave, go ahead. Remember, you will be in Transnistria which is not a safe area. It's better to be safe than sorry."

I received this email from David R., my contact person and a missionary in Moldova. It was less than 48 hours before I was to leave on my second trip to this beloved country.

Although Transnistria, a separatist group of people located on the east bank of the Dniester River in Moldova, broke away from Moldova in 1990 and declared itself a state, it is not recognized by Moldova or the international community. Many who live there want to remain loyal to the ways of the former Soviet Union, including Communism. There is a strong, active KGB presence, together with the persecution of Christians. The people have their own currency, government, passport, and border. Yet, to the outside world, they do not exist! No wonder David gave me that reminder.

It all started when…

James, my husband, said one afternoon in April 1998, "Barbara, I think you need to consider going back to Moldova."

"You do? Really? You *really do* think I should go?"

"I really do."

I am quite certain my eyes lit up and my heart started thumping as a big grin spread across my face. Now that James had planted the possibility in my mind, there was no more rest until I knew what God had to say about it.

"God, what do you think about my going back?" I prayed.

As I delighted myself in Him and read the Bible, it seemed His answer was, *Go! Encourage the believers.* I was a bit overwhelmed.

The question I asked Him next was, "How do I do this, Lord?"

In His own gentle way, God said, *Barbara, you've always trusted me in the past when I called you to go overseas. Trust me now.*

With awe and brokenness I simply prayed, "God, I do trust you, but you will have to lead me every step of the way."

I didn't hear an answer, but I felt His calming peace come over me. I knew this was my answer.

Since there was no team going at the time I planned to go, I asked several friends to go with me. None of the ones I asked could go. "Oh, God, no one can go," I prayed.

His reply, *I will go with you. You will not be alone. Now, will you trust Me completely?* Again, the awe and wonder of the greatness of God overwhelmed me.

I bowed my head. "Yes, Lord, I'll trust you with everything."

It was truly amazing. God brought to my mind every step of the way I had traveled before. I saw the corridors in the airports, the ticket counters, the waiting areas, and even the bathrooms. You see, my biggest fear was not going alone to Moldova, but the process of getting through the borders of Transnistria. But God even worked out those details so that David R. picked me up at the airport and brought along Oxana, my interpreter, who would stay with me. Praise the Lord!

I'd be living with Rasita and her family in Tiraspol, where I had stayed during my first trip. They lived about two hours southeast of Chisinau, the capitol of Moldova. Since I'd be spending the first night in Chisinau, James suggested I try to purchase bulk foods for the church.

I emailed David about this and he responded, "It's expensive, but you can buy sacks of beans, rice, flour etc. at the Bazaar. Let me know, and I'll get a van to transport the food for you."

While in Tiraspol, I planned to work with the Russian deaf congregation, teaching them how to share their faith, study the Bible, and do prayer-walking. For over two years, I had searched diligently to find a Russian sign language book. So far, it had been impossible to locate one. While I sign in English, it doesn't help me sign in Russian. Part of my dream for this trip was for the deaf people to help me learn some Russian sign language. This would allow them to minister to me, raise their self-esteem, and give them confidence in sharing the Gospel with others.

On this trip I wanted to teach conversational English classes to various age groups, as well as Bible lessons, songs, games, and activities for the children. I also had prepared studies on fear, anger, and unforgiveness for the ladies' groups. If I could get clearance, I hoped to return to the women's prison to speak there.

That was my plan; but I was aware that all of it might change.

David and I corresponded for months as he helped me prepare for my first solo mission trip. We discussed Bible lessons, discipleship training, the two currencies, daily interpreter fees, cost for lodging and transportation, getting across the borders, and anything else that might keep me safe.

The first time I had gone to Moldova, I had taken a youth team. All the arrangements were made for us, including getting us across the borders into Transnistria. We still had complications, but I was with a group and didn't have to pay attention to all the details, as I would need to do on this trip.

I'll be honest. I was terrified. Getting to Moldova and then into Transnistria was more complicated and dangerous than a "simple" trip to Europe.

A few days before I left, David asked me to bring some training materials, various foods, and books for him. A relative of his would overnight the books to me, if I agreed. He had been so helpful to me, I wanted to help him, too. So I agreed.

I already was packed within my 40-pound suitcase limit and ready to go when his materials and books arrived. Oh my! There were so many…and they were quite heavy. David told me I would be allowed 70 pounds per suitcase. I knew I couldn't manage a 70-pound suitcase, my 40-pound bag, and my backpack, but I did as he asked. It would be difficult, very difficult. It would make clearing customs harder. Transporting all of it around the airport would be challenging. Even though I'd rent a cart, getting on the shuttles at the airstrips would be nearly impossible.

August 18, 1998, finally came and it was time to leave. Several families from the church my husband pastored came for lunch. They traveled with us in the church van to the airport. It was a meaningful and loving send off.

Before boarding my plane, we joined hands and prayed

together. As soon as I kissed James goodbye and started my walk toward the plane, I felt the presence of the Lord come upon me in a mighty way. It was a very strong assurance that I was completely under His care and in His protection. God proved this to me over and over during the entire trip.

I found my seat and, to my surprise, discovered that the three seats next to me were empty. This arrangement was a gift from God because four days earlier I had been diagnosed with severe tendonitis in both feet. The doctor said not to walk, and to keep my feet elevated. During eight hours of flying, I had the blessing of keeping my feet angled up on the seats next to mine.

Another delight about sitting in this particular seat, was that several of us chatted with each other during the flight. I talked with a woman from Denmark at the end of the row. When she found out that I was a missionary, she wanted to know why I was going and what a missionary does. I had the privilege of telling her why I was going and all about why I believed in God, salvation, and Christianity. She had never heard any of these things before.

The woman sitting behind us was from France. She spoke up and said, "I didn't mean to eavesdrop, but I'm a Christian, too!" The woman from Denmark was shocked to find two Christians in one place. This was her first time to meet Christians. Between the two of us, we got to share how we came to know Christ, who God is, and answer her questions. The woman from Denmark was grateful, thanked us for telling her, and said she had some new ideas to think about.

Through those conversations, a mother and her daughter from Budapest, who sat nearby, also started asking questions about God. We talked and talked. When they heard I was going to Budapest for three days at the end of my trip, they adopted me for the rest of the flight and told me all about their country. Talking with nationals before I got there allowed me to better understand Hungarian culture. Before we parted ways, my adopted plane friends also got me through the whole process of customs in Amsterdam. Once again, this was God, providing for my needs.

I arrived in Budapest and found out I had a seven-hour layover. An email from my travel agent had informed me I'd be given my ticket for the flight to Moldova at the ticket counter. I wanted to check in early so I could relax and not worry about it. However, when I got to the counter and asked for my ticket, there was no record of my reservation. The counter attendant was sorry and said, "Come back in six hours, at 5:15 P.M. Ask for Leo. Maybe he'll have an answer."

Maybe?

So much for relaxing!

There wasn't much I could do at the airport because of all the baggage I had. My full cart of suitcases made me conspicuous, and I felt like a walking target for theft. I was afraid to leave the waiting area for my flight, but the few times I walked around I noticed a man following me. I purposely went different routes to see if he continued with me. He did. This made me nervous, so I walked with groups of people as much as possible.

The wait was stressful because I didn't know if there'd be a ticket for my flight into Moldova. What would I do if there was no ticket? I couldn't speak any Hungarian, so how would I understand the announcement for my flight? I needed to eat something…but how? All that luggage kept me from going very far to look for a food kiosk. And if I left, I might lose my seat and have to stand for hours, which would not help my tendonitis.

God had directed my steps so far. He promised He'd be with me. Even though I was afraid, I had to keep trusting Him. And I did.

After five hours of waiting, I desperately needed a restroom. Unfortunately, restrooms were located on the first floor of the airport, and there was no elevator. With the extra suitcase to lug around, it was impossible to get to the lower level. I prayed, "God, *please* show me someone trustworthy who will watch this luggage for me so I can get to a restroom." Immediately, He directed my attention to a woman and her husband sitting in a corner. They were from the U.S. She listened to my request. "Certainly, we'd be happy to watch your luggage," she said and smiled. When I returned, we had a great chat. I discovered the wife interpreted for the deaf in her church.

"Oh, that's wonderful!" I exclaimed. "I used to work with the deaf at a former church and I loved it. For part of this trip, my purpose is to train and teach my deaf Moldovan friends." Now, she was the excited one. We rejoiced together over our shared love for the deaf population.

Oh, my goodness. Had all of these specifics just happened? No way!

This was The Almighty God's awesome intervention and the quick answer to my prayer. Then God doubled the blessing with a precious time of fellowship and encouragement from this couple. God is good. Hallelujah!!

At 5:15 P.M., it was time to find Leo. I whispered another quick prayer, "Lord, I need a miracle of getting my ticket into Moldova. Amen."

I stood in the check-in line for 20 minutes. At 5:35 p.m. the miracle came. I stepped up to the ticket counter and asked the man behind it, "Are you Leo?"

"I am," he replied. "Are you with Bryan Tours?"

"Yes," I said. "They booked my ticket." I gave him my name and told him where I was going.

He turned to the counter behind him and picked up the ticket with my name on it. "Here you go," he said. "It was recorded under a vegetarian meal. That's why there was a problem."

Thank you once again, God.

I gave him a big smile and a hearty "thank you," and he checked in my bags, then nodded and pointed me to the gate.

Moldova, here I come!

Sitting on the plane before we took off, I prayed, "Oh, God, you are amazing. I am overwhelmed with all the blessings and how well you took care of me. Thank you for all the miracles you gave me today. Amen."

Tears at the Border

Moldova, 1998

———◆———

OXANA LEANED OVER THE FRONT SEAT and gripped my upper arm, "Quick, Barbara, give me the pack you're wearing and some money. Keep your head down and your eyes closed. Whatever you do, don't speak English." She looked at Boris, then back at me. "And, you'd better pray the whole time too."

My fingers trembled as I squeezed open the latch to my fanny pack, took out some money, and gave her both. She buckled the pack around her waist. I didn't understand the why, but the fear in her voice made me realize my life was in danger. *God, please help me trust her....*

David, my contact in Moldova, had arranged for Oxana, a lovely 20-year-old university student, to stay with me at the hotel. She also would interpret and travel with me during my two-week visit.

After we had checked out of the hotel, we met David in the lobby and he introduced us to Boris, a local carpenter. Boris would be my van driver today, and would return in two weeks to take me to the airport when I left the country.

Boris held out a calloused hand and gave me a gold-toothed smile. "*Hah-lo.*" He bent over and said something to Oxana.

"He wants you to know he doesn't speak English," she said. I nodded and gave him the okay sign. Through Oxana's interpreting, however, we were able to communicate quite well.

Boris dropped Oxana and me off at the street market bazaar and left to park the van. Stuffed right in the middle of an already crowded downtown, the Bazaar was surrounded by tall buildings that looked like huge white fences. Bus doors hissed as they opened and closed. Trolley cars stopped and started, and sent sparks flying like mini bolts of lightning as electricity flowed through the overhead cables. Kiosks, the size of a photo booth in an American mall, were squashed side by side along the sidewalks. Chickens squawked in their cages, and vendors called out in harsh voices, determined to coerce people to buy their wares.

It was only 9:00 A.M. and yet the market bustled with people young and old pushing through the crowds. An elderly woman waddled by trying to find the freshest vegetables for that night's dinner. Her heavy, blue-checkered bag bulged with potatoes, carrots, beet tops, and a bunch of celery sticking out the top.

Oxana pointed to the bulging bag. "That lady is probably going to make borscht tonight. We also call it 'red soup.' Have you eaten borscht?"

"Oh, yes, Oxana. I love it. My Russian teacher taught me how to make it," I replied.

Oxana and I walked until we came to a potato kiosk. I selected six potatoes from the pile. The woman at the kiosk took two away and slid forward two rotten potatoes. The stench was awful.

"*Nyet*," I said and slid them back to her.

She shoved them back toward me and said something harsh in Russian. I didn't understand the words, but I understood the message.

"*Nyet*," I said more firmly.

The woman stomped her foot and glared at me. Then she picked up my four potatoes and her two rotten ones, stuffed them into a bag and thrust them into my stomach. She raised her bony hand as if to slap me, then, lowered it with an outstretched palm expecting money.

"*Nyet*!" I said, frustrated that I didn't know enough words to say more.

I glared back at her and took the two rotten potatoes out of the bag and set them down hard on the counter. She tried once again to grab my bag and insert the rotten potatoes.

I plopped the whole bag down on the counter, looked her right in the eyes, and emphasized, "I don't want rotten potatoes." Then I turned and walked away.

She screeched out a string of blistering words.

"Oh, my!" Oxana covered her mouth and blushed.

I jerked to the right. "What'd she say?"

"You don't want to know." She shook her head and avoided my eyes. "It was nasty." She grabbed my elbow and whispered, "Keep walking, and fast."

"Oh, Oxana, here I prepared to buy all this food, and I can't even buy six potatoes!"

"Don't worry," she said. "I'll help you. She patted my arm and guided me through the narrow aisles. More than once I bumped into a crate or person as we shoved through the mob of people. Vendors snatched at my clothes and tried to get me to buy their wares. The smells of fried bread, sweat, roses, and dill assaulted my nose. Children darted between us. This place exploded with energy, and I loved it! I couldn't look at everything fast enough. As if she read my mind, Oxana nudged me and said, "I don't get to come here often. Amazing, isn't it?"

I nodded.

Boris returned and motioned for us to follow him. We squeezed around vegetable and flower kiosks. I jumped back as a squawking chicken flew against its cage and tried to peck me. "Whoa! That was close," I laughed. Boris laughed, too.

Boris turned toward me. "What do you need to buy?"

I glanced at the small quantities of goods in the kiosks. "I'm looking for big sacks of flour, also rice, beans, sugar, and dry oats. But I don't see any."

"You want hundred-pound tow sacks?"

"Can I get that much food here?"

He rubbed his chin and nodded. "Yeah, we can get all you want, but we need to go to the back of the market." With a jerk of his thumb, he indicated an area behind the kiosks.

"I'll go find a wagon, Barbara. Don't leave this spot, and hold on tight to Oxana. You're the only foreigner here, and I'm concerned that people are too interested in you—and maybe even your purse."

Oxana stepped closer and smiled as she hooked her elbow through mine. "Don't worry. Your purse will be safe between us now."

While we waited for Boris, we watched an old woman shuffle by us and then sort through a bin of hard bread. She smiled to herself as she tucked a crusty loaf under her arm and counted out lei to pay for it.

A few minutes later, we heard the flatbed wagon before we saw it. *Boomp-boomp-squeeeak, boomp-boomp-squeeeak.* Boris had borrowed an old, rusty wagon to use for an hour. He waved and gave a two-finger salute. "Okay, ladies. Now we shop."

He pulled the long wagon in front of us, making an easy path for us to follow him through the marketplace. Feeling a little braver now that Boris was back with us, I smiled and waved at some of the vendors sitting behind their counters. I was thrilled when some of them chose to smile or wave back at me. Children played hide and seek between the vendors, and lazy dogs stretched out under tables trying to stay cool in the shade.

The first vendor we encountered pounded the table and shook his fist several times at Boris. At last they negotiated a price for 400 pounds of flour. Then the vendor turned to glare at me. It was the same way with the rice, beans, and sugar vendors. None of them were happy with us.

Oxana grabbed my hand. "Come on, Barbara, hurry, let's go."

"*Oi!* Those guys were difficult." Boris wiped his forehead with his shirtsleeve. "Need anything else?"

"Not much." I glanced at my list. "Dried pasta, fruits, vegetables, herbs, and toilet paper."

Boris grinned in obvious relief and cracked his knuckles. "Okay, good. This won't take long. Oxana, you take Barbara over to the garden foods, and I will load these sacks into the van. Hold onto her tightly and get her good prices on the food." He left to load the van.

Oxana grabbed my hand and guided me through the passel

of plump, head-covered babushkas selling sunflower seeds, shoes, and scarves. Pressing through the throngs of shoppers, we headed to the garden corner of the Bazaar. By the time Boris got back, we had a bushel of peaches, some lemons, dill, 20 pounds of pasta, and 48 rolls of toilet paper. Several people murmured among themselves, pointed at us and then frowned at our conspicuous piles.

While we waited, I prayed this food would make life easier for my dear friends in Tiraspol. They, with all of Moldova, had gone through a horrible drought the previous year. Everyone had suffered and many died from starvation. Because they had treated me with such love and care during my last trip, I knew they would share this food with acquaintances and strangers alike.

Little did I know that my friends would not accept most of the food. Instead, they asked me to give it to the church to feed the local street orphans who came to the church daily for meals.

We soon heard the familiar rattle of the flatbed. Perfect timing. Sweat ran down my driver's face as he trudged through the bazaar and pulled the creaking wagon. "Tired, Boris?" I asked.

"*Dah,* a leetle, but I am strong." He raised his arm and made a muscle. "I will rest when I drive."

Oxana and I chatted as we walked to the van, but Boris was quiet as he pulled the wagon. He kept looking behind, then to the right and left of us. He stopped so fast, I bumped into him. He blurted out, "Barbara, I'm afraid we have problem when we reach the border."

"Why?"

"Because so much food," he explained. "It's not usual here." He rubbed the back of his neck and continued. "When we reach the border, guards will question us and might not let us cross over. The sacks are behind the front seat, under the windows and covered with a cloth. All the curtains are closed, too. We have trouble." He shook his head. "I know it."

"I can sit on the sacks and spread my skirt," Oxana motioned toward the van. "That'll help hide some of them."

"Okay," he told her and scuffed his shoe back and forth in the dirt. "That might work."

"Boris," I said. "I'm curious. Why *do* you have curtains over the van windows? This is strange to me."

His lips tightened into a straight line. "For safety. People want rides. When citizens see an empty vehicle, they block the road and often push or circle the car. Sometimes people get beaten, robbed, or even worse, have their car stolen." He crossed his arms and took a deep breath. "The other problem is the border guards. They want to make their lives better, so the guards look for something to take from you." He tapped the side of the van door. "Look what we have here…it is *so* much! Entitlement is big problem in Moldova, so we use curtains to hide things."

"And another thing," he looked behind him then bent closer to me. "You are American. Might be very dangerous for you."

"Oh, I understand now. It might be dangerous, Boris. But, God provided the money for all this food and the good deals we got at the bazaar. He *will* get us through the borders."

"Hmph." Boris slapped his hands on his hips. "How do you know, Barbara?"

"Because *God is God*," I looked him straight in the eyes. "And He does *great* things."

He blew out a quick breath and shook his head. "I hope so."

"Then let's pray about it. You drive. I'll pray, and Oxana will interpret."

"Dear God, you provided the money for this food. Thank you. Now I ask you to put a shield of protection around our van and this food inside. Please blind the eyes of the guards to this precious cargo and help us get across these borders. Amen."

"My friend, I know you are worried about these sacks of food. A thousand pounds *is* a lot, but…I, um, still need to buy more…about 25 gallons of water for Oxana and me. Is it okay?"

He paused, then his face relaxed and he grinned. "Okay, no problem. I'll take you to Green Hills Market. It's on the way. It's a European store, and you can buy everything there."

I lowered my sunglasses and peered over the top. "It's getting late. Do we have time to stop at a restaurant? I'll buy lunch for you and Oxana."

His eyes lit up and he gave me a lopsided grin.

The Green Hills market was delightful. It was probably the most modern place I would see while I was in Moldova. There were rows of cosmetics, lotions, and perfumes; chips, cookies, and cakes; stationary, greeting cards, and pens. There also was imported Belgian chocolate, Italian Tiramisu cakes, and clean fruit and vegetables beautifully displayed. I wanted to look around more, but I could tell Boris was hungry. He was looking at the huge selection of meats and cheeses at the deli counter in the back of the store.

I loaded my cart with water. Out of the corner of my eye, I saw Boris lick his lips as he stared at the meat in the deli case.

"Barbara, do you think we can buy food here and eat it along the way?" His stomach rumbled before I could answer. I quickly covered my mouth to hide the laughter that wanted to burst forth.

"Oh, sure. Great idea. Get whatever you want."

Boris chose a loaf of hard bread, a large salami, bottled tea, water, and Cokes. "Too much?" he asked and pointed to the food.

"No, it looks good."

The scent of cooked apples and cinnamon filled the air. The baker leaned over and slid a tray of flakey turnovers into the display case.

I motioned to Oxana. "Come here a minute. Smell these."

She leaned over the case and sniffed. "Mmm, makes my nose happy."

"Pick out any three and surprise us, okay?"

Her eyes widened. "You mean we get dessert too?" she squealed.

"If you want it," I winked and gave her a hug.

A vigorous nod up and down was her silent, but loud, answer. I laughed. "Get big ones!"

"Oh, this is such a treat." She giggled and shot Boris a shy smile. "It's absolutely wonderful." Boris smiled back and gave us the thumbs up.

"I've never had this much food at one meal before," Oxana looked down. When she raised her head, there were tears about to spill. She lowered her voice, "How much of it can we eat?"

I wanted to cry when I realized they'd been hungry before. I didn't want to embarrass her, so I said, "Eat all you want, Sweetie. We're celebrating."

"Celebrating what?" A puzzled look came over her face.

"Uh, you, me, Boris, and our new friendship. Okay?"

"Okay with me." She turned back to the pastries and sniffed again. "Mmm. Smells so good."

I paid for our purchases and picked up the sack of drinks. Oxana carried the treasures: bread, salami, and pastries. Boris loaded the five-gallon bottles of water into the back of the van. Oxana plumped up a sack of beans and got comfy. She handed me the bread. Twisting off hunks, I gave one to her and another one to Boris.

Boris laid his bread on his lap, reached under the seat, and pulled out a dirty knife. After he wiped both sides of the blade across his pants, he cut a big chunk of salami and reached over the seat to hand it to Oxana. He grinned and cut a second hunk for me. Then with a wiggle of his brows, cut a big slab for himself.

Oxana brought the meat to her nose and inhaled its fragrance before she licked her lips and took a huge bite. She closed her eyes and slowly chewed, savoring the flavor. "This is so yummy."

Although the van was comfortable, I dreaded the sweltering ride ahead. The last time I had been in Moldova, my older, superstitious van driver wouldn't allow us to ride with open windows. He said people feared getting sick or dying if fresh air blew on them. In fact, some of them have locks on the windows, so they can't be opened. Boris was different. He was young, maybe 25. We rolled down the windows and let the air slap our faces and blow through our hair. *Yay!*

During the three-hour ride, we saw cows grazing in pastures. I stuck my head out the window and mooed at some on the hills. Oxana joined me, and both of us mooed at these fine, black and white beauties. Boris shook his head and snorted at us. We looked at each other and laughed even harder. Like best friends, we were comfortable in each other's presence. Giggling, we bit into our crusty bread, and then brushed the crumbs off of our laps onto the floor. We drank our hot Cokes, savored our apple pastries, and licked our fingertips afterwards.

"Will you tell us about life in America?" Boris swerved to avoid a pothole.

"Sure, what do you want to know?" I glanced his way and expected the usual questions about music, sports, or fashion.

"What about the roads," Boris scratched his head. "Are they smooth, or torn up like ours?"

"And how much does bread cost?" Oxana interjected and rested her chin on the back of my seat. "Is it easy to buy?"

Both wanted to know how often I ate meat and if it was expensive. I had learned on my last trip to Moldova that meat was expensive, and Moldovans rarely ate it.

I didn't mind the questions, but I don't think they realized how powerful their questions about basic survival and everyday life were. I stopped laughing as I thought about how many times they had probably gone to bed hungry. I felt tears rush to my eyes and quickly turned my head. I wrapped my arms around my stomach and softly moaned. Now I understood the depth of their past hunger. Had they lost family members during the drought? My heart broke. It was all I could do not to double over and weep for what they had endured. I suppose my face reflected that sorrow, because Boris stopped laughing, too.

Boris pushed back the hair that kept blowing over his eyes. Thinking he had done something wrong, he said, "Barbara, I'm so sorry. You asked to go to a restaurant, and I didn't take you. Now you seem disappointed. Look at how we're treating you, riding along and eating in the van like this. Are you offended by such a lunch?"

I looked at Oxana with tears in my eyes, then over at Boris. "Oh no, no, I am not offended. I am very happy to be with both of you. I just was thinking about something else for a moment. I'm okay, guys."

"Are you sure you're not offended?" He chewed his lower lip. "I mean, aren't Americans used to nice things?"

"Isn't this a nice thing?" I asked. I laid my hand on his forearm. "I'm with new friends, having a delicious lunch, and riding in a van with the windows down. How much better can it get?"

Neither Boris nor Oxana said anything.

"Hey, you two." I twisted to look back at Oxana. "I've got an idea. Let's call today's celebration a van-nic. It's like a picnic, only in a van. What do you think?"

"Good idea." Oxana lifted her Coke bottle high in the air.

I raised mine and tapped the edge of hers. "To the van-nic."

"To the van-nic," Boris and Oxana cheered. Boris gave me that lopsided grin again and his shoulders relaxed.

Poking her head over the seat, Oxana looked back and forth at us. "Well, guys, since we're celebrating our new friendship and having a van-nic, may I please have more salami?"

"Of course! And while you're at it, Boris, cut me another piece, too. We're celebrating, right?"

"Right." He honked the horn once and sliced both of us another chunk of meat.

Patting her stomach, Oxana sighed and flopped over on the sack of beans. As she finished her last bite, she said, "Ooh, it's like heaven to me to have so much food. I could eat and eat and eat."

Boris interrupted and reached his hand toward me. "Barbara, we're close to the first checkpoint. Pray! Now!"

"God, it's up to you. Please help us. Amen."

It was then that Oxana asked for my fanny pack and some money. I heard the fear in her voice and knew I had to trust her.

We rolled up the windows, and a minute later drove up to the checkpoint. Oxana and Boris climbed out of the van and hoped to distract the guards so they wouldn't look inside. I kept my head down and prayed. Fifteen minutes passed, then 20.

Oh, God, what is going on? I prayed silently.

A moment later I felt the warmth of the sunshine leave my face as a shadow covered the window. The temptation to open my eyes and look out the window ripped me apart inside. As if this person heard my thoughts, I soon felt the warmth of the sun return.

Soon afterward, the van door squeaked open, the seat bounced, and the engine roared. We moved forward. My heart squeezed in my chest, and I didn't move. *Oh, please, Lord, protect me from whoever's driving this van.*

When I felt I no longer could hold my breath, Boris spoke, "Barbara, now you can open your eyes."

I breathed a sigh of relief and shouted, "We made it across. Hallelujah!"

Boris shook his head. "No! No hallelujahs yet. We still have two checkpoints before we get to the border. Both are worse than this one."

I shifted to look back at Oxana. "What took you so long?"

Boris slammed the steering wheel. "It's my fault. There was a problem with my passport."

"Yeah, and they almost didn't let us cross," Oxana squeezed her hands together. "We had to pay some taxes, and we used your money, Barbara."

I looked in the side mirror and saw her wide eyes. "How much money?"

Oxana tucked her chin and lifted her eyes. "Thirty lei," she said and hesitated, "a month's salary. And it really wasn't taxes. We kind of had to pay a bribe, or they wouldn't let us cross. But they did give us a receipt!" She tipped her head and waved a paper.

"How much is thirty lei in dollars?"

"About seven dollars," she replied.

I smiled at her in the side mirror. "It's all right, Sweetie. We made it through." I heard a relieved sigh and then watched her face as it formed into a shy smile.

"Boris, now what?"

"We pray harder." His eyes were intent on avoiding a tree growing in the road. "We have 20 minutes until the next stop." He tapped the steering wheel while Oxana twisted her long hair around her finger.

I reached out to touch both of them. "It's okay, friends. Don't worry. We *will* get through this. My church in America is praying for me." As a gentle peace came over me, I adjusted my seatbelt and relaxed, trusting that God was in control and would also handle this next checkpoint.

There were no cars in front of us when we pulled up beside the second, dilapidated guard station. Oxana and Boris opened their doors. The officer signaled for them to remain inside. A second guard prowled around the van and tried to see through the curtains. When he got to my side, he tapped on the glass and motioned for me to roll down the window.

I smiled. "*Dobray dien.*"

The guard nodded and attempted a, "Hah-lo, good afternoon," back to me in English.

My jaw dropped, and then I smiled.

He smiled back. "Do you have Bible?"

My mind flashed to my luggage. It was stuffed with Christian literature. "Yes." I swallowed hard and pointed at him. "You want one?"

He studied the ground, then raised his head and stared long into my eyes before he gave a curt nod.

"Oxana, please open my bag and get me a Russian Bible."

I gave it to him.

He took it with both hands, gently held it to his lips, and closed his eyes. When he opened them I noticed they were shining with tears. The gratitude reflected in his eyes pierced my soul. "I dreamed always to have such a book." He pulled the Bible close to his chest.

"*Malinky?*" I asked.

"*Dah.*" He raised two fingers and moved his hands trying to indicate his children's ages.

Turning sideways, I motioned. "Would you get me two of those children's books, Oxana?"

She did, and I passed them through the window.

"*Spasiba. Oh, spasiba bolshoy.*" He thanked me over and over as tears now flowed freely down his cheeks and splashed onto his uniform.

This man risked his life to ask for a Bible, Lord. Please, please have mercy and protect him.

His comrade walked over to see what he held. "Bible?" I asked while I studied his hardened face.

He jumped back and spat on the ground. "*Nyet.*" Then he repeated it for emphasis.

He gestured for us to show him our papers. When he saw my forms from the Baptist Union of Moldova, he grunted his disgust and thrust them back at me. With narrowed eyes and a jerk of his hand, he dismissed us to pass through.

Boris shifted the gears and the van shot forward.

"Hallelujah!" I raised both arms.

"Not this time." Boris rapidly shook his head. "The last checkpoint is the worst. It's the one before crossing the border into the former communist Transnistria territory. Pray fast. It's only a block away."

We slowed down at the checkpoint, but the guard waved us across the border.

I heard a gasp. "They didn't stop us! We got through. This never happens." Boris's lips trembled and his voice cracked. *"Now you should shout hallelujah!"* He wiped his eyes with the back of his wrist. "This is miracle. I have seen miracle today. *Slava Boga*! Glory to God! God did this! We sing now and give thanks to the Almighty."

Oxana stretched over the seat and patted my shoulder. "You have no idea of the danger back there. We might have 'disappeared'…forever." She wiped her eyes on the edge of her skirt. "It's my first time to see a miracle, too."

"Hallelujah," I shouted. "The food will be delivered!" This time Boris didn't stop me.

We rolled down the windows, honked the horn and clapped.

Oxana reached over the seat and threw her arms around my neck. I hugged her arms. There was no doubt—the presence of the Lord was with us.

With tears running down her cheeks, Oxana quietly sang "Amazing Grace." Boris joined in, and so did I.

One hymn, two languages, and three voices united in praise to the Almighty.

The bazaar where we purchased the bulk foods

A trolley bus crowded with people coming to the bazaar

The 1,000 pounds of bulk food in the back of Boris' van

Oxana during our salami and bread van-nic

Boris, my van driver, after getting me to Rasita's house

Reunited

Moldova, 1998

WE FINISHED SINGING, and then I said simply, "Thank you God for hearing and answering our prayer about getting across the border. We love you. Amen."

We only had about 30 miles left to drive before we arrived at Rasita, Zhanna, and Igor's house in Tiraspol. I showed Boris the address, but he didn't know where it was. I began to see familiar sights as we pulled into town, but I still didn't know where we were going. We stopped at a gas station to ask directions, but no one there had heard of the address. We asked a lady standing on the corner if she knew where it was. No luck with her either. We stopped several more times and asked people, but no one had heard of it. This is strange, I thought. I've been to this house. Now where is it?

"Barbara, do you know where we're going?" Boris asked.

"No, Boris. I don't." And then I told him to turn right.

He looked over at me with a surprised look, "I thought you didn't know where you are going?"

"I don't, but God does, and I feel like He is leading me to go this way. Go straight for two blocks." He did, and I said, "Turn left. Keep going. Boris, turn here," I motioned with my right hand. "Go up there. Now straight ahead. Wait, that's it! That's Rasita's house," I yelled.

Boris looked at me like I was crazy. "Are you sure?"

"I'm pretty sure. Let me out. I'll yell and bang on the gate. They know my voice and they will open the door. Here, Oxana, take my camera and get pictures."

I flung open the door and jumped out of the van. Then I started pounding on the iron security gate and hollering, "Rasita, Rasita, it's me Barbara. It's me. Rasita. Open the door."

I heard the front door open, then the sound of running feet pounding on the sidewalk.

I heard Rasita shout in Russian. "Barbara! Barbara! I'm coming." Then I heard the key scraping in the lock and turning. The rusty, eight-foot gate swung open.

"Rasita!" My legs couldn't move fast enough as I ran into her arms. We held on tightly to each other and cried, smothering each others' faces with kisses.

Then the front door swung open again, and Zhanna ran out wearing the fuzzy brown bathrobe I remembered so well.

"Barbara! Barbara, you came!" she cried. She jumped up and down and pulled me into a bear hug. She covered my face with her tears as she lovingly rubbed my back. "You're here! I knew you would come. I knew it." We squeezed each other tightly while Oxana snapped pictures and tried to wipe away the tears that wouldn't stop running down her face.

I was bursting with excitement and sputtered out everything as fast as I could. "I brought food to share! God did a miracle for us. We got across the border! Oh, I'm so happy to see you!" I hugged Rasita again, then Zhanna. Then I linked my arm through both of theirs. "Where is Igor?" I asked.

"He's taking a bath!" Zhanna replied.

Just then the door flung open and Igor ran out. "Barbara! You're here." He ran to give me a hug. All four of us hugged again. What a reunion!

"Oh, I'm sorry. Let me introduce all of you," I said. I pointed to my left. "This is Oxana, my interpreter, and this is Boris, my van driver."

I shyly looked to the ground and then back up. My heart was about to burst open with joy, and I smiled happily. Then I said, "Oxana and Boris, I want you to meet my very dear and precious Moldovan family: Rasita, her daughter, Zhanna, and her son, Igor."

A happy Rasita and me, meeting again after two years

Meeting Zhanna again after two years

Igor and me, the day after I arrived

Treasures in the Garden

Moldova, 1998

THE WINTERS IN THIS SMALL COUNTRY between Romania and Ukraine are brutal and harsh. Death is imminent without compote, surviving is a challenge. Sometimes the pipes freeze and no water is available anywhere. When this happens, compote, a boiled drink using apricots, grapes, apples or cherries, is the only liquid available until the spring thaw. The fruit needs to be prepared and boiled within 10 to 15 hours of harvesting or it will spoil. Making compote is essential, taking precedence over everything . . . including sleep.

In their letters, Rasita and Zhanna, had used phrases such as brown and crispy, dusty and scorching to describe the drought in Moldova the previous summer. They said most of the vegetables and fruit rotted or shriveled on the vine. They had no harvest. Everything that breathed struggled to survive. Young and old suffered from dehydration; others slowly starved to death. It was brutal, horrific, catastrophic. People still grieved. Tears had rolled down my cheeks as I read these letters. No matter how many times I wiped them away, they kept coming.

I noticed how different it was this year. As I walked along the country road, gravel crunched under my feet as I skirted around potholes in the road. Tree limbs sagged under the weight of swollen apricots. Red apples dotted yards. There was no brown only the red, green, purple, and orange of tomatoes, sweet peppers, grapes, and melons growing on trees in vacant lots, hanging over fences and behind closed gates. Children skipped and chased butterflies and their mamas laughed again. Excitement flowed like electricity at the anticipation of going to bed each night with full bellies. I took a deep breath and smiled. What a blessing to realize no one would die because of thirst or starvation. This year, God had provided.

The church where I taught at the children's camp was several miles away. When I reached home, I noticed Rasita had harvested all day. The tables were piled with corn, peppers, tomatoes, onions, and cucumbers. Apples and melons rested in battered pans under the sorting table, and buckets of apricots overflowed near the steps. Vegetables grew upward from the corners of the yard and on top of vines. No land or space was wasted.

A flowered oilcloth was spread on the outside table and dinner was ready. Before eating, I carefully splashed my face and rinsed my hands under the garden hose, then sat down to eat the vegetable soup Rasita had prepared. I also took a big spoonful of the tomato and onion salad, had a portion of her scrumptious fried potatoes, a piece of bread, a slice of homegrown watermelon and a glass of cherry compote.

I ached to rest longer, but I also was in a hurry to help. Rasita already had gathered wood and started the fire. She told me she didn't have time to eat, because tonight we needed to make compote before the fruit went bad. If we didn't get it done, they would have nothing to drink until the next harvest.

Rasita poured buckets of water into a deep metal vat that rested on an iron grate. She piled wood under the grate and stoked the fire often to keep the water at a boil. With the back of her arm, she wiped her brow and shoved back her hair. The dullness in Rasita's eyes reflected her exhaustion. I wanted to hand her a cool cloth or a drink of water, but she didn't stop for a break. Instead, she bent over and dragged the pile of wood closer to the fire.

The gallon compote jars, when full, weighed nearly nine pounds. Rasita had three jars of fruit and water prepared to boil. With slow and careful movements, she tightened the lids and lowered the jars into the spitting vat. If the jars didn't explode during this process, they would seal themselves, and the mixture would settle into compote overnight. If a jar shattered—and it happened often—there was glass to sweep up, the chance of getting burned, hours wasted and the grief of losing half a bushel of fruit. I didn't know the cost of a jar, but I knew Rasita's daughter Zhanna, a doctor, made $10 a month. I could only imagine how much of a tragedy it would be for a compote jar to break.

Zhanna got home at dusk. She grabbed an apple, and pointed to two loaded tubs of apricots. In between bites, she said it would be easier to pit the fruit if we moved our stools and the apricots closer to the tomato patch where the ground was level.

While Zhanna ate her apple, I decided to get started. I attempted to lower my wide girth onto a three inch high, dinner-plate sized stool, but I overshot it. I flailed over backwards, and yelped with surprise as my arms and legs swam in the air. I hit the ground hard with a thud and sprawled out flat in the tomato vines.

It happened so fast, I didn't know what to think. Although dazed, I heard Zhanna and Rasita as they pushed aside pans and climbed over squawking chickens, buckets, and hoses trying to find me in the dark. "*Varvara!* (Barbara)," they shrieked.

I couldn't see them, but started to giggle. They almost stepped on me, but saw my arm waving through the vines like a white flag of surrender.

My laughter continued. Zhanna tugged on my arms and Rasita pushed from behind until they got me on my feet. My biggest concern was squishing the tomatoes and ruining the crop. Their concern was me and that I was okay. I flung clumps of squashed tomatoes out of my hair, out from under my arms, and off my dress. The fire cast a glimmer, and I saw the horrified look on their faces as their eyes swept over me. I probably looked like a tomato monster.

Relieved that I was okay, Zhanna raised her hand to cover a grin. She pulled my arm through hers and led me back to the pitting area to settle me on the stool. By this time the sun had set. There were no street lamps or flashlights. The fire cast shadows through the trees that made them look like sea creatures dripping with wet seaweed. I reached into the tub and grabbed an apricot. Zhanna showed me how to squeeze until the seed popped out. I tossed the seed into one bucket and the fruit into another.

At times, I felt worms crawling up my arms. I gagged just thinking about it and hoped I hadn't thrown any of them in with the pitted fruit. Juice dripped down my arms and the apricot seeds felt wet and slimy. It reminded me of when I was a kid and visited a haunted house on Halloween. We had to stick our hands into a bowl of peeled grapes that was supposed to represent plucked eyeballs. Going into another room, the guides had us put our hands into a bucket of cold, wet spaghetti, which was meant to give the feeling of dead worms. I cringed at the memory as I flung these very real worms into the bushes.

There was no breeze in the garden. It was as hot as a desert and as humid as a tropical rainforest. We three roasted as the compote boiled. Sweat dripped down my face and stung my eyes. I licked my parched lips as the smell of those juicy apricots reached my nose. I was so thirsty. Oh, how I craved a sip of something wet. But Rasita and Zhanna didn't stop for a drink, so I didn't either.

My dress and skin were sticky with apricot juice and my hair smelled like tomato sauce. The mosquitoes were persistent as they sucked on my ears, eyelids, neck, and toes. I itched something fierce. "Go away you blood-sucking pests." I swatted the air to no avail. "Leave me alone!" Those mosquitoes ignored my pleas. *Humph, probably because I told them in English, not in Russian.* With renewed vengeance they continued to gnaw on me until I was swollen in misery. My skin burned, and my body hurt from the fall. I was exhausted, frazzled and ready for a good cry.

Even after smashing the valuable tomato plants, these hard-working people trusted me enough to work alongside them in their garden. They shared everything they owned with me, including their hearts. Our friendship was growing. At that moment, I realized my friends loved me more than their life-sustaining garden. Contentment filled me, and it was a greater emotion than my suffering and misery.

I glanced over at Rasita as she tended the fire. Her hair was plastered to her head and sweat poured off her face and ran down her arms. Like a hawk watching its prey, she stared at the jars in the boiling water. Every few minutes she leaned down to poke more wood under the vat. It was difficult and she burned her hands several times. Rasita wrapped old towels around the canning tongs. Then she began to lift the heavy, scalding jars from the bubbling water. My heart almost stopped as I watched her struggle to stand upright. The water lapped and splashed up and over the sides of the vat. I sucked in my breath as I watched her.

Oh, dear God, help her.

She settled the scalding jar on a pile of folded towels, then stretched her back. My breath whooshed out.

Thank you, God.

I had tasted apple, cherry, pear, and apricot compote during the week. Oh, my, it had quenched my thirst better than ice cold lemonade. However, now that I had experienced the process of making it, I decided to drink only one glass at a time, no matter how thirsty I got. Rasita and Zhanna would be happy to give refills, but I knew to drink more would come at a high price for my friends during the winter when the compote was almost gone.

During my two-week visit, Rasita had cooked for me, walked me through the forest to the church so I wouldn't get lost, and had even massaged my shoulders. Many mornings she woke me up with a kiss on the cheek and a hearty, "*Dobraye utra,*" good morning in Russian. What a gift of love she gave me to be treated so royally! On more than one occasion, the emotions in her eyes had pierced my soul as we tried to communicate with one another. Our vocabulary was limited, but our hearts talked non-stop!

Sometime after 2 A.M. when we finished work for the night, I wiped my hands on my dress and sank down on the wooden bench near the fire. I patted the bench and waved for Rasita to join me. I pointed to her feet and motioned for her to put them in my lap, so I could massage them. She shook her head no, then cast her eyes downward.

"*Gryazny*," she mumbled.

She was embarrassed because, she said, her feet were dirty. They were grass-stained, covered in mud and chicken dung. I shrugged and motioned again. With a long sigh she sat down, leaned her head against the wall, and slowly raised her calloused feet to my lap. I massaged her swollen ankles and toes with great care. This sweet lady with silver front teeth and turquoise-blue eyes followed my hands as I rubbed each foot. I looked up and smiled at her.

When I stopped rubbing her feet, Rasita slowly got up, reached out and held onto my shoulders. When she stood back, I saw tears running down her cheeks. I could see by her eyes, she had more to say, but the language barrier prevented it. She patted my face and kissed my cheek over and over again.

Zhanna watched all of this from the metal stool where she sat. She got up and ran to my room to get my Russian dictionary. By firelight, she searched to find just the right words. Blinking back tears and biting her lip, she said, "Barbara, beautiful."

Zhanna's words touched me deeply. I made a place for them in my heart, and I later wrote her words in my journal.

Tears poured down my cheeks. In a few days I would leave Moldova, realizing I probably would never see these beloved people again. Our three hearts communicated through our eyes and the love and respect we had for each other. My soul hurt like it was being ripped out. I had fallen in love with this land and these dear people, and I never wanted to forget this evening.

The real treasure in the garden was not the valuable fruit and vegetables, nor the life-saving compote that we made. It was the experiences of love and unselfish care we gave to one another.

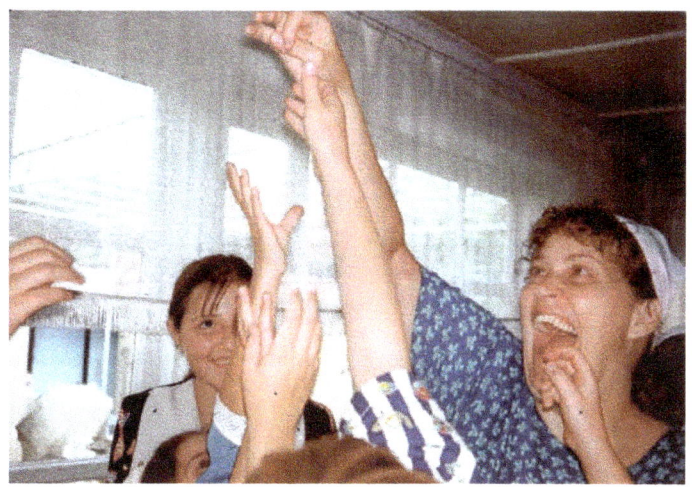

At the children's day camp

One of Rasita's delicious dinners with the food from her garden: borsht, cucumbers, spaghetti, veggie patties, bread, and fresh peaches, pears, and oranges

In the garden before I became a tomato monster

The work area for preparing foods and making compote

Getting ready to prepare the apricots

Zhanna drinking apricot compote from the previous year's supply

Three Hours Later and I Almost Died

Moldova, 1998

MY NIGHTMARE HAD BECOME A REALITY. I had trusted God and now I was in the middle of what I wanted to avoid: people and exposure.

It started that morning when my bedroom door slammed open and banged into the wall. I whirled around from making my bed. Zhanna came in grinning and waving swimsuits in the air. Oxana followed.

"Barbara, come go swimming with me in the Dniester River." Oxana interpreted. "I want to be sunburned for my wedding in two days."

"Sunburned? Why?"

Zhanna blushed and glanced at the photo of Sasha, her fiancée. She ducked her head and in a soft voice said, "To look healthy and pretty in my wedding dress."

"I didn't bring a swimsuit."

"No problem," she said. "Guests left extras."

She shoved a navy blue and white, two-piece swimsuit into my hands and tossed Oxana a turquoise one-piece.

I looked down at my plus-sized body and flung it back. "Nope, I'm not parading this thing in public."

"Please go with me. It'll be fun. You'll see." Zhanna said, and threw the suit back. "We're going to go change. Be right back."

I shut the door and looked up. "This is ridiculous, God. I can't wear this. Remember, I'm here in Moldova as a missionary."

Then I heard His quiet, inner voice that I knew so well. *Wear the swimsuit, Barbara.*

"No, God, please. I can't. You'll be embarrassed…and so will I."

Trust me, daughter. I will be glorified.

"I don't think so. There's not much to it."

Barbara, will you wear it?

"Oh God, I don't want to. Please, no." I groaned long and loud, then, "Okay, Father, I'll do it." I looked upward. "But only because I trust you and you promised you would be glorified." Holding up the two-piece, I shook my head and sighed. With a lot of grunting, tugging, and a final yank, I squeezed my girth into that skimpy suit. It was not a pretty sight.

The door opened a crack and Zhanna peeked in. "Ready?"

I shrugged. "Come on in." I turned and faced the wall to avoid her eyes.

Zhanna spun me around. "Perfect," she said. "Let's go."

"*Nyet*, not perfect," I mumbled and grabbed my blouse and skirt and pulled them over the swimsuit. I slung my backpack over my shoulder. "Remember, I have to be at the prison at 3:00 for Bible study."

"Don't worry. We'll get you there on time," Zhanna said as she shoved me out the door.

We walked about 45 minutes down the dirt and gravel road before we got to the bus stop in the center of town. Within minutes, the air reeked of gasoline as the packed bus squeaked and hissed to a stop. The three of us and two others pushed through the doors and pawed the overhead bar trying to get firm grips. During the bumpy and sweltering ride, boney knees of strangers jabbed my legs, and stinky armpits in my face made me gag as we jostled in the aisle. There was no air conditioning and, as always in Moldova, the windows were sealed shut.

At last the torturous ride was over and we staggered off the bus. The sultry, polluted air smacked me in the face. We walked a few blocks until we saw a beach crowded with swimmers. "Zhanna!" In panic I stopped and begged, "Please, please promise me we'll go to a private area, so no one sees me in this swimsuit."

She slipped her arm through mine and smiled. "I promise."

We walked past all the swimmers and hiked for an hour through the forest. I raised my arm to wipe the sweat that ran down my brow and into my eyes. Mosquitoes buzzed around my head. I slapped at them, but they were happy and content to chew on me. My thighs rubbed and my feet hurt. By this time, we had traveled almost three hours. I was miserable, hot, and ready to crawl under a tree to die.

"Barbara, up ahead. Look," Zhanna pointed and said, "a private area near the beach."

"Oh, thank goodness." My wilted body was ready to cool off.

We chose our spot. Oxana spread our blanket over the sand and we dropped our backpacks. I yanked off my headscarf, skirt and blouse and hobbled over branches and rocks to the water. Cool mud squished between my toes as I waded out into the riverbed. I plunged right in and swam out about 50 feet. Oh my, it was refreshing.

"Hey you two, come on in." I motioned. "The water feels wonderful."

Did Oxana and Zhanna dash into the water? No! They did not. They splashed a little water around their knees and stood there. Oxana giggled and said, "We're not coming in. We don't want to get our hair wet, since we're going to the prison."

No amount of coaxing could persuade them. Swimming out further, I enjoyed doing somersaults. Suddenly I felt something like a hard punch in the stomach. Then my legs twisted painfully underneath me. The river churned furiously as my body became distorted and was sucked downstream. Fear sliced through me. I struggled for air when my head came out of the water. Although I kicked, fought, and tried to swim across the rip current, it carried me further into the swift-moving water.

"Oxana! Zhanna!" I sputtered. "*Pa-ma-gee-ti-ya*!" They laughed and waved.

"Help me! I'm in trouble." I splashed and was sucked under again. The fear in my voice escalated enough to make them hurry down the beach toward me. Water swirled around me as I tumbled down the river. It ran up my nose and down my throat. "Oh, God, help! I'm drowning." Death was coming. I accepted it. However, all I could imagine was my dead body being washed ashore in that gross, tiny swimsuit.

A strong, vice-like jerk pulled at me with no warning, and my body was freed from the rip current. The water was peaceful again. My heart pounded and I gulped in pockets of air. "God, that was you, wasn't it?" I burst into sobs. My tears mingled with the river water, and I knew I wasn't going to die.

At last, Oxana and Zhanna were only a few yards away and ran into the river. Both of them grabbed my arms and pulled me to my feet. My legs wobbled and I couldn't stop shaking, but they held me tight. Clinging to them, I cried and rested my head on their shoulders. They rubbed my back and stroked my hair to comfort me.

At the sound of voices, I took a deep breath, lifted my head and opened my eyes. No, no, no, not this! A large gathering of swimmers stood there watching us. I'd tried to avoid them on our earlier hike through the forest. Now I stood in front of them with my jiggling rolls of fluff exposed in that horrible swimsuit. People whispered and pointed at us. With Zhanna and Oxana's help, I stumbled out of the water, but felt the stares of the crowd while I trudged the long, half-mile walk back to our spot.

I collapsed onto our blanket and draped a towel over my head and face. Perhaps, this would block out my memory of the gawkers.

A few minutes later, Zhanna scooted across the blanket and gave me a poke. She whispered, "Barbara, don't look. A man got off his bike and is sitting by the bushes watching us."

I removed the towel from my face and sat up. "Are we in danger?"

"I don't think so." Zhanna chewed her lower lip. "But he's a sick man and is showing himself."

Although uncomfortable, we pretended he was not there while I prepared for my Bible study. As I thumbed through

Ephesians, my attention was drawn to Chapter 4, verses 17-24.

"Yes! That's it!"

Zhanna dropped her book and Oxana looked over at me.

I handed my Bible to Oxana. "This passage talks about holy living. Read these verses in Russian, Sweetie, as loud as you can."

Oxana took a deep breath and shouted out the Scriptures.

With the Lord's authority let me say this: Live no longer as the ungodly do, for they are helplessly confused. Their closed minds are full of darkness. . . .They have given themselves over to immoral ways. Their lives are filled with all kinds of impurity. . . .Throw off your old evil nature and your former way of life, which is rotten through and through, full of lust and deception. . . (Ephesians 4:17-20 NLT).

We heard the bushes rustle and a twig snap. The middle-aged man stood, picked up his bike and rode off.

That inner voice of the Holy Spirit came to me again and whispered, *Now, I have been glorified.*

Yes, Lord, you have. Hot tears spattered onto my lap.

"Why are you crying, Barbara?" Oxana asked.

"Just a minute." I raised my hand and bowed my head. *God, please forgive me for my pride and for doubting you this morning. I am so sorry. And, Father, thank you for saving my life. Amen.*

I looked at my precious friends, and continued to wipe my cheeks. "Dear ones, I need to tell you something. God promised me He would be glorified if I would wear this swimsuit. I couldn't understand why. It made me angry and I felt embarrassed. I love God and I trust Him. Even though I didn't want to, I chose to obey Him. You see, the Bible states in Proverbs 16:7 *a man plans his way, but God directs his steps.* This is what happened here just now. God knew this man would come here to watch us. He used my obedience to share His message of holy living."

Zhanna nodded.

Oxana dabbed her eyes with the edge of her towel. "I've never experienced anything like this," she said. "That man heard the truth, and maybe for the first time." She reached for my hand and squeezed it. "Barbara, God is here with us. Indeed, He has been glorified."

Zhanna's wedding

Reuniting With the Deaf Believers

Moldova, 1998

I**T HAD TAKEN TWO YEARS**, but I finally was back in Moldova. On Sunday when I walked into the church, my deaf friends quickly left their seats and ran to give me hugs and kisses. Once again we were a tangle of necks, arms and tears. Oh, how I loved them!

Oxana told the deaf interpreter to have my friends meet after the service, so we could make plans for evening Bible studies.

Tuesday night came, and my deaf friends had invited some of their friends, a total of nine.

We waited and waited, but their interpreter never came. Now what would we do? How would they understand? I saw the looks of sadness in their eyes, as one by one they hung their heads in disappointment. One of the deaf men who read lips very well said he would read Oxana's lips and interpret for the others. He signed our plan to the deaf, and they were eager to try it.

Oxana and I quickly changed our presentation. I spoke and used a flannel graph to show the story. Oxana translated into Russian, and the deaf man read her lips and signed back to his friends. None of us knew if this process would work.

But it did!

The visuals of the flannel graph made the story come to life. At the end of the story, the deaf clapped and all began signing at once. The man who signed to them could speak, just not hear. He said for the first time they truly understood the Gospel message. They were excited. As arms waved in conversation, they laughed and wiped tears as well. It was one of those moments when God showed up. Oxana and I added our tears, too.

Next, I told them, "Tonight I'm going to teach you how to be a missionary."

A man named Ghemma signed to the speaking man, "Oh, but we are deaf and not respected. We can't be missionaries."

"Oh, yes, you can," I said as it was translated and signed back to him.

"How can we do this?" he signed.

"I'm going to teach you how to do prayer-walking. Afterward, we'll go out into the community and practice."

They were amazed they could be missionaries, and were eager to learn how.

"Do you pray?" I asked.

Heads nodded "yes."

"Can you walk?"

Again heads nodded "yes."

"Good! Now we're going to walk around the neighborhood and see what to pray about, okay?"

As we entered the courtyard of the church, I told them we could pray for people coming and going to the church. "We can ask God to keep them safe," I said. "We also can ask God to bring new people to hear the Gospel message."

We started walking, and a military truck full of soldiers passed by. "Friends, we can pray for peace and protection. We can thank God for the soldiers patrolling to keep us safe."

They nodded.

"Now, see that little boy over there with no shoes? We can ask God to protect his feet until he can get shoes." There were nods of enlightenment.

Suddenly, they understood. One woman pointed to a group of people walking. They decided to pray for them. Hands and arms moved rapidly as prayers were sent to heaven. Then another man pointed to a playground. They decided to pray for safety for the children. There was nothing for me to do but enjoy the blessing of watching them be missionaries. We walked and prayed for over an hour. The joy on their faces told the story. They understood and obeyed.

I later learned two of the people in our group were hearing. They worked in the church kitchen, but they wanted to learn how to be missionaries, too. They had to leave early, but on the way back, they stopped two people on the road and invited them to church.

Our animated group got back to the church to decide on the next time to meet. They talked among themselves and asked if I would come at noon on Thursday to the shoe factory where all of them worked, and share the messages I had shared tonight. Oxana and I agreed.

However, when I saw them two days later, the factory would not allow it.

"You can be missionaries at your job because you know how

to prayer walk," I encouraged them. "During your breaks, look around you. See who might be sad or lonely or in pain. Then pray for them. You can tell them about the story you understood tonight." Again they nodded.

"Yes, we can be missionaries. Now we know what to do."

When Oxana and I came back for the next class, the deaf had planned a surprise party for us, including gifts and food. Oh my, what a delightful blessing! I received a Christian plaque with a message, tomatoes, fruit strudel, bread, and a lovely pair of red decorated, shoes from their factory.

One of the ladies even made hot tea. We decided to eat the strudel. Then Ghemma again gave me a lovely oil painting. He was quite talented and had painted the large mural at the front of the church. The painting he gave me was a replica of the one on the church wall. It was a mountain scene with flowing water beside it. Peaceful and lovely.

To my delight, the deaf gave me one of my dreams and taught me 10 Russian sign words. I was thrilled.

Then each person taught me their sign name. In sign language every person has a symbol or sign identifying who they are. They showed me their separate symbols and waited patiently while I tried to sketch them, so I would remember them. For example, Marsha's sign was a hand sliding down her nose to represent her glasses always sliding down her nose. Oleg's sign was to point under his nose; representing his mustache. Marina's sign was an arm across her brow, representing an old lady.

We talked and laughed and had a grand time of fellowship. We ended our meeting with Oxana using the flannel graph and teaching about Jesus taking care of His lambs. We answered questions about Jesus and the Bible, then prayed. These precious people were so kind and loving toward me. What a glorious experience it was! Oxana was blessed, too. "Now I know how to be a missionary, too. I can do this anywhere," she whispered to me.

The most important part of this experience was my deaf friends understanding they were valuable in God's Kingdom. They were important, could learn, and, like others, also be missionaries.

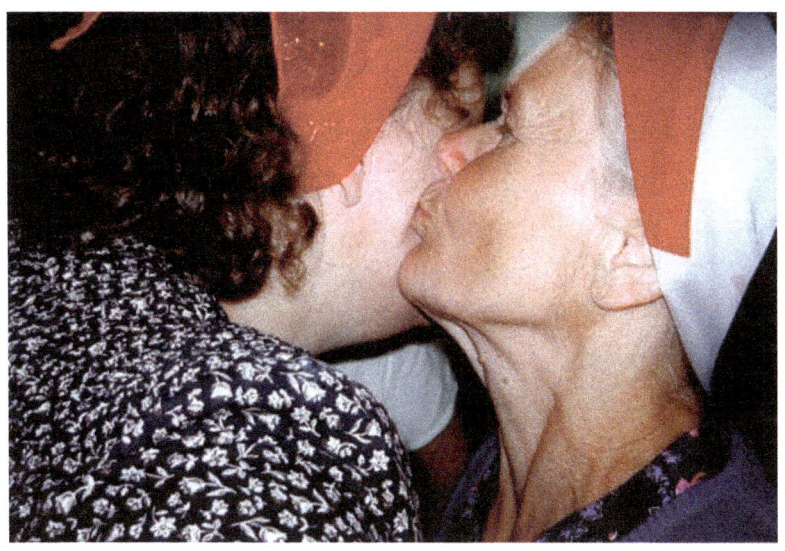

A deaf woman giving me the customary hug and kiss

The deaf learning how to prayer walk

The children practicing a song in sign language
to sign for the deaf on Sunday

Russian Sign Language Alphabet

Poor Chicken

Moldova, 1998

I*t was my last day in* Tiraspol…a bittersweet time for me. I was ready to see James, but also knew I may never see my beloved friends in Moldova again.

Our 90° weather had vanished overnight and we woke up to a cold and dreary day with pouring rain. Oh, it was so cold! Rasita lent me a sweater and handed Oxana a rain coat. With my black skirt, beige sweater, flowered headscarf and bag, I certainly looked like I belonged in the community.

Before we left for church, Rasita wanted to tell me something. With a look of love and tenderness in her voice, she said, "You are very loved by the people here. It's because you are simple and not proud as some Americans. You love everyone—all kinds of people. You talk with everyone and they know it. You don't leave anyone out. The people love you very much."

Oh, my goodness, those words…I could not comprehend such precious words. I loved these people dearly, as well! Although life is different, I will never be a stranger there. I know the land, the people, have shared in their joys and sorrows, have walked their streets, ridden their trolley buses, visited their stores, carried bags, and worn head scarves. I have eaten their food, visited in their homes, hugged their necks, and shared Jesus together with them. It has been the richest experience for me, and I have grown deeply because of it. These dear, precious people will always have a special place in my heart.

After Rasita's very kind and humbling words to me, Oxana and I pondered which way to walk to the church that morning. The short way meant walking through part of the woods, down a rocky path and across a two-foot deep creek with a homemade bridge. This was not your usual wooden bridge. It was made of old tires, bedpans, a ladder, and other pieces of tin. Not a fun bridge to cross even in the best of weather, but it definitely made the trip to the church shorter. During both of my trips to Moldova, only once had I slipped off a tire and plunged my leg into the green slime. But Oxana and I both remembered the event well, and, since it was raining, we decided walking several miles along the puddle-filled gravel roads would be best.

All week the children at the church worked hard to learn a song in English and in sign language. Our deaf friends would be surprised as well as thrilled! The church was packed that day. Even with the heavy rain, the people walked for miles to attend and bid me farewell. Without a doubt, I would leave part of my heart in Tiraspol when I left the next day.

I hadn't felt well all morning, but attributed it to being tired. However, I got worse instead of better. Before the service, the pastor asked me to preach a sermon prior to the children doing the special music and signing. "Preach?" Oh, dear! *Help, God. Please give me Your words, so I can do this. Amen.*

The Lord gave me Proverbs 16:9 (NLT) as the scripture: *We can make our plans, but the LORD determines our steps.* I talked about coming to church with the right attitude, forgiving others, not being self-centered, bitter, or angry. I explained that we don't have to carry these sins with us; we can repent anytime and be free.

During the service, I had to dash through the rain to the outhouse. Ooh, not doing well…. I was able to preach the sermon and lead the children in their special song for the deaf, but immediately afterward, I ran back to the outhouse. By now, I had chills, nausea, and diarrhea. Ooh…not good. So I wouldn't keep disturbing the service, I stayed in the nursery and watched the service through the window.

At the end of the service, the pastor stood and asked, "Where is Barbara?" I waved from behind the nursery window. Then he said, "Thank you for coming to us again. Thank you for your work and messages. You are always welcome. Next time also bring your husband!" He smiled and said, "The church has prepared to sing your favorite song: 'Sing the Whole Earth to the Lord.' " I stood as they sang and joined in singing, but I felt worse than ever. They concluded the service by singing to me in Russian: "God Be with You 'Til We Meet Again." My heart broke, and the tears flowed. It was beautiful. Next, all the church members formed a line to say their goodbyes. They handed me gifts and candy and were generous with hugs and kisses.

And what did I do? I started throwing up everywhere. Someone got me into a chair and held a bag under my mouth, but we discovered it had a hole in it. I remember a lady mopping up the puddle in my lap while I continued to throw up and wave goodbye to these precious, beloved people. *Oh dear, is this the way they will remember me?* I kept apologizing.

All was not lost, however. The pastor came over to me and kind of grinned, "Did you drink the water?" he asked. "Don't worry; other Americans have thrown up, too."

The real blessing came when he drove Oxana and me back to Rasita's where I promptly ran to the outhouse! I never could have endured the long walk in the downpour.

The pastor went back to the church, but returned several hours later to drive me to a church service in Bendery, about 40 minutes away. I shook my head. "There is no way I can go," I told him. "I am so sick."

"But the church is packed and they are waiting for you," he said. "They remember you from your last visit."

"I would love to go and see them again. I'm so sorry, but I'm too sick."

He returned to his home and brought back Luda, his wife, who was a nurse. She took my temperature. It was 103°.

"Do you have any of the 'pink stuff'?" she asked Rasita.

Rasita didn't, but she went to several of her neighbors and borrowed some. Luda checked the medicine and said, "This will work. Take it every four hours. It will kill bacteria, but it's bitter."

And it was!

Trying to stop some of my chills, Rasita covered me with two wool blankets and a duvet, but I couldn't quit shaking. My dear, 20-year-old Oxana lay down on the bed beside me, so I could have some of her body heat. She rubbed my arm and said over and over again, "Poor chicken, so sick. Poor chicken." That unselfish act of love and care deeply touched my heart. *God, thank you for this unique and compassionate person, who not only is my interpreter, but also a dear friend. Please bless her, Lord.*

It was a rough afternoon, and after over a dozen trips to the outhouse, Rasita brought in a chamber pot for me to use. She joked and said, "You have been to the outhouse more than you have been at church." These dear people loved me in health and in sickness. They were the hands and feet of Jesus to me every moment of both trips. It's no wonder I dearly love them.

A little later in the evening, Oxana came to my room to check on me. She said, "I need to tell you something…Rasita killed a chicken for you to eat."

"What? A chicken? Which chicken?" I said.

Sadly she shook her head. "It's your favorite one. The one we kissed goodnight every evening!"

"My friend?" I gulped.

She nodded.

"Oh, Oxana. I can't eat my friend or anything else," I said. "You'll have to eat it."

"Me?"

"Uh, huh," I shook my head. "We can't waste the chicken. Pretend you don't know which one it was," I told her.

Later when dear Rasita brought me the cooked chicken and some vegetables, I had to sadly decline. My stomach wouldn't allow food right then. I felt horrible that, out of love, she sacrificed and prepared one of her skinny chickens for me. With great sadness in her eyes, she allowed Oxana to eat it. And dear Oxana, out of her love for me, ate it.

You never know what you'll experience on the mission field, but you have to be flexible, or you won't make it.

By morning, "the pink stuff," whatever it was, had worked. I still couldn't eat but felt much better. Boris, my van driver, arrived at 8:50 to drive Oxana and me across the borders. He also took me to the airport, where I would catch my flight to Hungary for the last part of the adventure.

The homemade bridge, the shortcut to the church

The long way to the church

At home, very sick, after saying farewell at the church

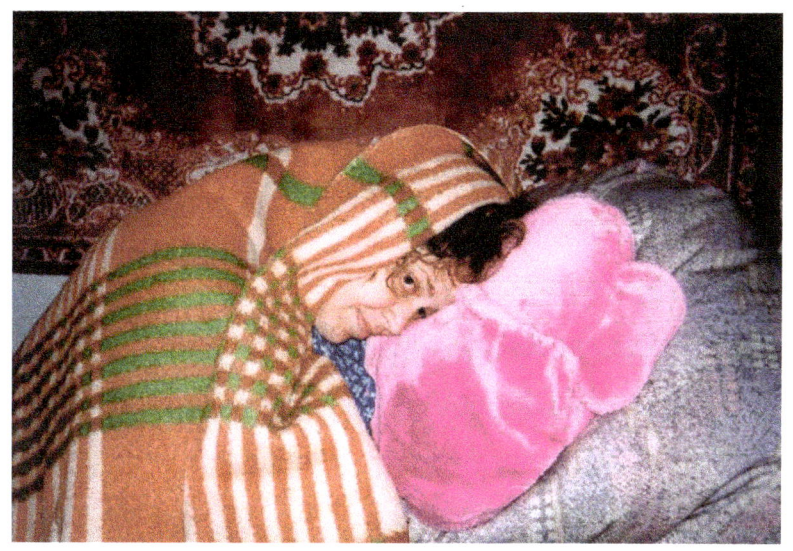

Wrapped in blankets after church.... Poor Chicken

The day after being sick, and the "pink stuff" had worked.
Our final farewell before going to the airport
for the flight to Hungary.

Hungary
1998

To the Potatoes!

Hungary, 1998

Boris got me to the airport in Chisinau, Moldova, but had to leave right away. It was a different terminal than what I remembered. It was packed with people pushing and shoving—all trying to get to their flights. It was hot, no air conditioning, no English, and I couldn't figure out what to do.

At just the right moment, however, God sent Mashie, my interpreter from my first trip, to help me get through passport control. She arrived less than 20 minutes before my flight to Hungary took off. Bless her heart! Since I had last seen her, she had married and was 8½ months pregnant. I could tell she felt miserable because she was sweating and her face was red. She also fanned herself with a paper to cool off because of the intense heat.

The man who was supposed to have taken me to Mashie's apartment for a visit, had decided he didn't want to do it. Oxana had tried to call him three times, but he never answered the phone. I felt horrible that I had no way to let Mashie know I wasn't coming. Thankfully, she remembered my departure time and came to me at the airport.

Our time was short. She kissed my cheeks and thrust gifts of a small, decorative vase and a CD of birdcalls into my hand. She wanted to give me these personal gifts so I wouldn't forget her. After I gave her the gifts I had brought for her, she grabbed my hand and quickly pushed and shoved through a long and crowded line. Somehow, she was able to get me a personal attendant who got me to passport control.

What a miracle that Mashie had come and helped, because at passport control I was told I was missing a document. The man waved me through anyway, and my personal attendant made sure I was on my flight to Hungary. Although my visit with Mashie was brief, the gift of her time was priceless to me. She probably paid a bribe to the attendant to take care of me. It all happened so fast I didn't know what really happened. Oh, but, how good it was to see her again! I never would have been able to get through customs in time for my flight without her help. I will always treasure those brief 20 minutes. *Thank you, Mashie, for your sacrifice of love and care for me.*

My flight to Hungary was delightful. There were only four passengers on board, and we were treated like royalty with extra smiles, candy, and mineral water. The stewardess served us a meal of chicken, pasta, salad, bread, and a brownie. The elderly man across the aisle from me struggled to open his food container.

"Would you like me to help you?" I asked as I smiled and motioned opening a container. With a look of relief and gratitude, he nodded and handed me his food. Later he held out his brownie. I smiled, opened it and gave it back. I was glad to do it. With only four passengers on the flight, it felt like a little family. We couldn't speak much, but we sure smiled often at one another. It was wonderful.

After arriving in Hungary, my next obstacle to conquer was to find the correct van to take me to my hotel. Oh, me of little faith. Why was I fearful now? God directed my steps to the minibus ticket counter. The lady at the counter spoke English. "Yay!" I got on the correct van, and 35 minutes later was delivered to the front door of my hotel.

This hotel wasn't near the center of town as was my hotel the last time I was in Budapest, so traveling out from this hotel might be a challenge. To do or see anything, I would have to catch a bus to the other side of town. That might be stretching my bravery a bit much, but I was determined to give it a try…or so I thought.

The next morning, I got up the courage to take a 25-minute walk around the back of the hotel and through the park. It was pleasant, but I didn't feel safe at all because I felt like I was being watched. Actually, I was scared and nervous. *Hmm, now what am I going to do for my three days in Budapest?*

God provided again!

When I got back to the hotel, I overhead a foreign lady asking in English about the location of a mall. On my previous trip, I had walked through a small mall, now I hoped to do so again. I stepped up to her, introduced myself and asked if she wanted to go together. She did. After checking the clock, we decided we didn't have enough time because she wanted to go on a bus tour of the city at 2:00 P.M.

"Would you like to go on the tour with me?" she asked.

"Sounds good to me," I said.

We signed me up for the tour. In the meantime, we took a walk, had a coffee, and got acquainted.

I told my new friend, Monica, about my recent trip to Moldova and how sick I had been the day before. She interrupted me and said, "Honey, we're having a worldwide conference of gastroenterologists. There are 2,000 of us here at this conference and 200 of us staying at our hotel. Whatever illness you had or have, one of us can fix you."

Now don't you just know God smiled at my jaw-dropping reaction of surprise? Father God had already paved the way for me to be at this hotel with all of these doctors. I believe it was one of the ways He was letting me know not to worry. He still was guiding my steps.

Monica and I got along quite well. She had been invited to this conference to present a paper on liver bacteria. We discussed our homes, families, and travels. She was from Chile but had traveled all over the world. This was her first time in Budapest, though. Since I had been there before, I suggested a few places to see, and after our bus tour, off we went! We had purchased our transit tickets at the hotel before we left for our walk. The hotel clerk told us to take the #8 bus to get us back to our hotel. During our walk, we visited the castle district, went shopping, and got more coffee. It was fabulous.

Monica really wanted a Spanish language book on Budapest. We had searched in every shop where we went, but there were none to be found. Finally, at our last stop, we found one copy hidden high on a shelf. "Monica, look! God provided!" I said and grabbed the book for her. She took it and gave me a huge smile.

After shopping in the underground stores, we located our bus stop and boarded the bus. But we couldn't figure out how to use the pay system. In English we discussed ways to get the ticket into the machine. None of our methods worked. An English speaker, sitting near the front of the bus, overheard our conversation. She got up and showed us how to use the machine. Not only that, but this kind woman listened for our stop and pointed us in the right direction to our hotel. We mouthed a grateful thank you as we exited the bus. Through the helpful woman, God again provided.

We went to supper at the hotel and thought we had ordered sandwiches. Imagine our surprise when we got turkey and French fries instead. Ha! We never did see the bread; the meal was good, though. We called each other's rooms several times during the evening trying to make plans for the next day.

I answered one of the calls and thought it would be Monica; but, to my great delight, it was my beloved James. After all these weeks apart, how good it was to hear his voice again! We chatted a while, then he said, "I might have some bad news for you. The airline you were returning on is on strike. You don't have a flight home. Instead of going through Amsterdam, you'll have to go through Germany. Bryan Tours made the arrangements for you."

"Oh, my! James, that's some challenging news! I'll need to change the time for my van back to the airport."

Truthfully, while a bit nervous about the change, I was excited about adding another country to my list of visited countries.

At 2:30 the next afternoon, Monica called from the lobby. She said, "My friends and I are ready and waiting for you to come do things with us. Can you go?"

"Oh yes. I'll be right there."

Juan Carlos and Celia, Monica's friends, were also doctors from Chile. They spoke very little English; but they were talkative and friendly. We all had a great time trying to find ways to communicate.

That day's trip was a boat ride on the Danube River over to St. Margaret's Island. Our hotel called a cab to take us to the boat dock. Unfortunately, the driver got lost and took us to the wrong pier. After getting directions, we walked at a fast pace to the correct pier and got on the boat only minutes before it was to sail. We had wanted to sit on the upper observation deck to better see the sites, but there were no seats available. Instead, we got the last four chairs on the main level. I had the joy of sitting next to a man from Italy, his three year old son, and the boy's "teddy bear."

The mini cruise was relaxing. I loved having the fresh air blow through my hair and in my face. It was refreshing after the six-block jaunt from the wrong pier. The sites along the river were incredible. We rode by the Hungarian Parliament building, the Buda Castle and the Chain Bridge. I looked as fast as I could, but it was difficult trying to squeeze all the beautiful sites into my memory as we sailed by them.

Once we got to the island, we walked around for several hours. We enjoyed seeing the varieties of flowers in fuchsia, orange, yellow, red, pink, purple, and more, as they blossomed in gardens and dotted cobblestone pathways. There were fountains, statues, and hedges sculpted in patterns, too. This place was a paradise in itself.

"Celia and I are hungry," Juan Carlos announced. "Who wants to eat?" He smiled when he received a hearty "yes!" from Monica and me. We tried to find a restaurant, but had no luck. They decided on an outdoor bar and hoped it also served food.

I had never been in a bar before and wondered what our church would think knowing their pastor's wife was in a bar while out of the country. However, there was no time to think about it because soon we were seated and a waiter stood before us.

The three of them ordered beers, and Juan Carlos, pointing to me, spoke up and said, "Coke Lite for Barbara." I hadn't even told him I didn't drink alcohol. He seemed to know. I was thrilled. Using Spanish, German, and limited English, Juan Carlos tried to tell the waiter we also wanted food. The waiter shrugged his shoulders and shook his head indicating he didn't understand any of those languages.

"Let me ask if he understands Russian," I said. "*Ga-vah-ree-tee, pa, Russke?*"

"*Dah,*" the waiter nodded and replied.

In my limited Russian, I asked if we could have four orders of French fries with ketchup.

"*Dah, yah-pah-nee-my-o.*" (Yes, I understand.)

I hoped French fries were what I ordered.

Minutes later our waiter came back carrying a tray with four orders of piping hot French fries and little containers of ketchup!

Yay! Oh, what a moment it was for me! I'd tried my Russian and it had worked. I was excited, and so were my tablemates. We all clapped and cheered because the waiter understood and I was able to get us some food. My tablemates lifted their beers to me and waited. Then I realized I was supposed to make a toast. I'd never done that before either. I lifted my Coke Lite. I didn't know what to say, so I pointed and said, "To the potatoes!"

A chorus of "To the potatoes!" resounded. We clinked our glasses and had a good laugh.

The potatoes were not cut in stick shapes like we were used to, but in small square cubes. It didn't matter to us. They were delicious. We enjoyed every single French fried cube on our plates. Ha!

We continued to laugh and chat, but who knew that while sitting at a table in a bar, I would have the opportunity to share the Gospel message? Apparently, Monica had told Celia that I was a missionary. Through Monica, Celia asked, "Would you tell me about being a missionary and also tell me about your faith and your religion."

After explaining what I did in Moldova, I told her about Jesus being God's gift to us. I talked about the cross, the resurrection, and that my faith was having a personal relationship with Jesus Christ.

She grabbed Monica and said, "Tell her to explain more—repeat everything again."

I explained that God sent Jesus to take away our sins. How Jesus was crucified on the cross and was resurrected, so that we might have life and be forgiven and have a relationship with Him. Celia nodded again.

With a thoughtful look she then said, "Your faith is more free and caring and not all caught up in rules like my religion. I like it."

For the rest of the afternoon, Celia continued to ask me questions about my faith.

After walking a bit more, Juan Carlos said, "Hey! Let's all ride the horse and buggy."

We loved the idea and flagged down a buggy driver. We took lots of photos of flowers! Then it was time to go back to the pier for our return trip. After a pleasant ride, once again enjoying the crisp, cool air on the water, we arrived back at the mainland. Here we walked for over an hour, up and down lots of steps until we located a place that sold bus tickets back to our hotel.

Monica was exhausted and went back to her room. Juan Carlos and Celia decided to look around the park. I went to the hotel restaurant where I ordered my first Hungarian goulash and Wienerschnitzel. It was different, but tasty.

While I was eating, Monica came back to the restaurant. She and the others wanted to invite me to their cocktail party that evening. After graciously thanking her for the invitation, I declined because I needed to pack for my early-morning flight back to the States. We hugged our good-byes, and I thanked her for including me in all the fun.

"Oh, I enjoyed it, too," she said.

I asked her to "please thank Juan Carlos and Celia for me and tell them how much I enjoyed meeting them."

She promised she would.

Even though I had a reservation for the flight from Budapest to Munich, when I got to the airport at 7:10, there was no record of it. Perhaps, God prompted the airline agent, because she decided to check again. Eventually she did find my name listed. Because of the airline strike and the need to use a different airline for my return to America, I was told to take the tram to the other airline terminal and get the transfer approved. At the other airline, the ticket agent worked for almost 20 minutes on my situation and finally handed me a ticket. *What a relief.*

By now, it was raining. I went back outside to catch the tram back to my terminal. At the ticket counter, wet, but happy, I handed the agent my ticket and had no further problem getting on the flight.

During the 1½ hour flight to Munich, I talked with Elise, my seatmate. She had just spent three weeks in the Atlanta suburb of Sandy Springs, Georgia. Many years before, I had lived in Sandy Springs for a year with Betty Durham, the woman I met in Israel. It was fun watching the surprise on Elise's face when I told her that. She asked what I had been doing in Moldova. I told her about my missionary work and some of the miracles God had done.

"That's interesting," she said. "Would you tell me about your faith?"

"I'd be glad to tell you," I said. It was another opportunity for me to share the Gospel message of salvation.

When I got to Munich to check in, I was told it was a full flight and I should wait to see if they could get me a seat. *Here we go again.* With only 10 minutes before the flight left, the agent called me to the desk. She started to hand me my boarding pass, but suddenly changed her mind and took it back. She filled out another pass. Then she said, "Here you go, I'm giving you a seat I think you'll really enjoy."

What had she done? She'd given me a seat in business class! "Oh, my goodness! Thank you! This is incredible. Thank you so much."

I'm sure my response made her as happy as her gift made me.

God had shown favor on me and I'm certain prompted the agent to upgrade me at the last minute. *God, this is another miracle. Thank you so much.*

My return trip was spectacular. I had a lovely gift in my seat consisting of a pair of slippers, an eye mask and several sweet-smelling toiletries. I turned to the older lady beside me and confessed, "I've never flown business class before. What should I do?"

She replied, "Just sit back, young lady, and enjoy the personal attention and pampering."

And you know what? I did.

They served me a three-course dinner, complete with a linen napkin and Godiva chocolate. I had headphones, a reclining chair with a foot rest, three feet of leg room and a 6-inch arm rest. Oh, my goodness. This was deeee-light-ful!

Then the stewardess said, "Oh, I forgot, you also have unlimited drinks."

I said, "Thank you. Just keep the orange juice coming. You have no idea how much I'll enjoy that."

Oh, God, You have blessed so much. I am not worthy to receive such a fine gift. But I am ever so grateful. Thank You.

As we talked during the eight-hour flight, Maria, the older woman beside me, told me she was from Austria, but now lived in Oregon. One of her questions to me was, "What did you do in Moldova?"

I said, "I was a missionary, helping people and telling them about God's love for them."

She wanted to know details and found my experiences interesting. I shared all the many ways God had taken care of me. Before she decided to read for the last two hours of the flight, Maria asked a final question, "Do you think any of your work made a difference?"

"Oh, Maria, yes. I believe that it did. God showed up in ways I never would have expected. I know these events will encourage the Moldovans, and it certainly encouraged my faith. I give Him all the glory for the great things He has done."

Monica, the gastroenterologist from Chili who befriended me at our hotel

The castle district, taken on the walk with Monica

Russia

2004

Unexpected Visits

Russia, 2000 & 2004

WHILE I HAD OFTEN PRAYED FOR NADIA, my interpreter on my first trip to Russia, I had given up on ever corresponding with her. Sadly, it seems that letters sent to Russia often disappear. Nevertheless, God is still the God of miracles, and He provided a precious miracle for me.

One fall, I spoke at a church about my trip to Moldova. Visiting that night was Eleanor, a woman who soon would be leaving for Russia. As we talked, she agreed to take Nadia's phone number with her to Russia, and a letter "just in case" she found my friend.

After her return, Eleanor told me that when she arrived in St. Petersburg, she dialed the number *and*...got Nadia!! *and*... Nadia worked in the building right next door to Eleanor's hotel! Nadia was thrilled to be remembered and immediately went over to the hotel to visit with Eleanor.

As a translator in a Christian school, Nadia had access to email! YES! Now we could communicate. I wrote her immediately.

In one of her emails, Nadia told me about a woman who

came up to her in a church she was visiting. "You probably don't remember me," the woman said. "I was in prison six years ago and you were the translator for the American group that came." Nadia remembered the day well and told me it was the time our group from seminary was there. I remembered that day, too. The woman told Nadia, "I listened and my life was changed that day. I'm a Christian now and serve in this church."

For years I had pondered the memories of Nadia and that prison experience. So often we sow seeds, but never see the harvest. I am grateful to God to be reunited with my friend and to know that our ministry really did make a difference. May God be praised!

Nadia's Visit in 2000

Now that I'd reconnected by email with Nadia, I wished we could have an in-person visit again. I didn't see how that could be possible, but apparently God thought it was important. For years my husband and I usually owed money when it came time to file our income tax, but in the year 2000, we got a generous refund. Maybe we could use this refund to pay for Nadia to come to America for a visit!

We presented the idea to her and told her we could pay for the plane ticket. She doubted she could get off work. Her boss, however, thought it was a great opportunity. He gave her time off, but said it would have to be without pay. God provided again, and she was able to get a reasonably-priced ticket. Since the flight was cheaper than we thought, we were able to give her extra money to cover her lost wages. Oh, God was so good and provided everything needed!

Our visit was delightful. In addition to all the talking,

laughing, and crying, we had a picnic at a local park, grilled hot dogs, introduced her to s'mores, and splashed in the creek. Another day we went thrift shopping, and she tried Mexican food afterward. Since we lived in Maryland at the time, we even went to Washington, D.C. because she wanted to see The White House.

Last of all, we gave her a surprise birthday party. We invited guests who brought presents. "Oh, but it's not my birthday," she said.

"I know. But you won't be here in August for your birthday, so we decided to have a party now to celebrate," I told her.

The surprise totally worked, and when the hidden guests popped out of a bedroom and yelled "Surprise," she jumped high and screamed loud. God was so good to provide this trip and wonderful visit.

Returning to Russia in 2004

But that's not all. In 2004, God allowed me to go back to Russia for a third trip, and spend time with Nadia and her family. What an adventure it was!

A year after her visit with us in Maryland, Nadia emailed me with spectacular news. After waiting for over 23 years, Nadia, her husband, Sasha, their two adult children and Nadia's mother had finally received permission from the government to move to a larger apartment. They had been crammed into a tiny two bedroom apartment. Now that permission had been granted, they quickly moved and got settled. It was easy to rejoice with her.

"What can we get you for your new apartment?" I asked.

"I'd love to have curtains for the bedrooms and living room," she replied.

"Maybe I can find them here, Nadia, and mail them to you. Tell me what kind you want and give me sizes."

Nadia had her artist daughter, Masha, sketch out and add color to the designs she wanted. She then mailed me the sketches.

James and I searched for two years and went to five different states to find exactly what Nadia wanted. When we finally found them, they matched the pictures perfectly! Were we ever excited! But how to get them there? We looked at every transport option for a year. However, from past experiences, we figured that if and when the package arrived in Russia, they would never receive them.

One day James blurted out, "I think you need to go back to Russia and deliver the curtains in person."

Wow! I wasn't expecting that. At that time, I had traveled by myself to China once, and I had traveled alone to Moldova the second time. Surely, I could go to Russia by myself, too. After talking with Nadia about bringing them in person, James and I decided I should go.

Since I was delivering curtains, we thought it would be helpful to take other hard-to-get items like vitamins, Ibuprofen, lotion, spices, peanut butter, coffee, underwear and socks for the family, etc. In addition to the difficulty of getting these items in Russia, finances were very tight for this dear family. Our prayer was that these gifts would make things easier for them.

And then there was my internal struggle: *Can I do this?* My Sunday School teacher, another Peggy, spent many hours talking with me about the decision of going or not going. Here's a portion of one of her emails to me:

> I'm glad you found some comfort in my words…and glad that you are following through with the Russia trip. I still

> feel that this is your destiny for this moment in time. It's exciting to think about what He is going to do in and through you once there.
>
> You have been given a special gift and privilege that all of us don't receive. I know we are all told to "go" but some of us receive a special call to go overseas and you are one, my dear.

If it had not been for Peggy's encouraging words, I might have backed out completely. I clung to what she wrote to me, but it continued to be a struggle.

I still needed to buy many things for the trip: a heavy coat, boots, a ticket, and so much more. And honestly, I didn't know where the money would come from.

God, this trip is one of absolute and total faith in you to provide. I am stepping out on the smallest limb. God, you have provided in the past, why is my faith weak now? Please give me wisdom. I can only do this trip by your mercy and grace. Please give me joy about going. Everything in my flesh wants to stay here. I am your servant, God. Take away my unbelief. Amen.

I shared this call to go back to Russia with my church, and I came home and cried and cried. It was a relief to get it out in the open. Then fear would smack me in the face again. I was scared. Could I do this? I think my fear was because I didn't know my purpose. James reminded me, "Your purpose is to deliver the curtains and other supplies."

When friends in Tennessee, where we now lived, found out I was going, they wanted to help buy the items. I was overwhelmed by their generosity. Not only did they purchase the items on my list, but also special treats like canned tuna, chicken, and beef stew. It would give my friends variety in food and maybe even fill their bellies for a change. What a blessing this was!

I planned on taking only a small rolling backpack for my clothes, but I would need to take two huge rolling suitcases for all the gifts. Memories of lugging the extra suitcase to Moldova and how difficult it had been came to mind. *Oh, God, I can only do this through you.*

Nadia told me conditions were very hard for them and would be for me, also. She said there might not be heat or hot water. When I got into my cold bed here in America, I wondered how in the world I would survive in frozen Russia. When I was chilled after my hot shower in the U.S., how would it be to have no hot water and maybe not even a cold shower there?

About six weeks before I hoped to leave, a miracle happened. One of the church staff ministers came up to me and asked, "Are you still thinking about going to Russia?"

"Yes, I am. I have all these supplies given by the people, but I still don't have money for the plane ticket."

He said, "Two families from the church know that you are called to go on the trip to Russia. They also know that you are supposed to go with our church group to China in May. They have given money, so all your expenses for the trip to China are already covered. Now you can use the money you intended to use for China to go to Russia."

The news left me totally speechless. I couldn't believe it. *Lord, once again you have provided. I don't know the plan, but I'll go as you lead the way. Your grace is sufficient, Lord, and it abounds freely. Thank you. Amen.*

With all the unknowns, *Russia, here I come*!

My concern now became about getting through customs

and having the gifts confiscated. It happens.

Going through immigration control was another miracle. Thankfully, there was no problem with my paperwork. As I walked to the line for my luggage inspection, I talked with Irina, a Russian woman who had been on my flight. I was next in line for the inspection, but the agent was dealing with another passenger. As Irina and I continued to talk, she motioned with her eyes to keep walking, so I did. The agent gave me a glance, but ignored me. I breezed through with no luggage search, so Nadia and Sasha were able to get all the gifts without anything being pilfered.

The day after I arrived in St. Petersburg, Nadia told me we had to go to a government office to register my passport. Was that ever a cold day! The wind stung our faces with an icy chill. The canals were frozen, and there was ice and snow on the streets and sidewalks. But we did have some sunshine.

We walked to the bus stop and waited for 30 miserable minutes; it never arrived. Then we walked to another bus stop trying to get to our destination. Once we arrived at the passport office, we tromped up three flights of stairs to a smoke-filled office where a very kind man helped us. He told us to come back at 4:00 to pick up my passport, and he gave me a map of St. Petersburg.

Laughing and talking, we left the building at 1:00 and had only walked a minute or so when some boys came up to us and asked for money.

"*Nyet*," Nadia said.

"*Nyet*," I also replied.

Immediately, they attacked us. Over 15 teenaged boys

surrounded us. They grabbed our arms and pinned them to our sides. One boy jumped on my back and began beating me. Another one looked me right in the eyes and unzipped my cross-body bag. As he worked on getting into my bag, I bent forward and was able to jiggle my arms loose.

"Pa-ma-geet-tia, Pa-ma-geet-tia," (Help me! Help me!) I yelled as loud as I could. In the meantime, Nadia was yelling "Help me! Help me!" in English. It's comical now because I yelled in Russian, and she yelled in English!

I raised my right foot and stomped hard on the instep of the boy on the right. Then I doubled over again to hold onto my bag. The boys continued to reach for my arms to keep me from moving.

The boy pawing around in my bag pulled out what he thought was a zippered wallet full of money. He held it up in front of my face and gave a haughty laugh.

Fortunately, someone saw the beating and muggers and blew their car horn loud and long. At last, the boys let us both go and ran off. Nadia and I stood there trembling and in shock. We didn't know what to do, so we stood in the middle of the sidewalk and held onto each other. Words were hard to find.

The experience was terrifying, but, in my opinion, we experienced miracles. At the last minute, I had worn a very heavy coat instead of the raincoat I had planned to take. The thickness of the coat protected me from the beating. I wasn't even bruised. Nadia said she wasn't hurt either.

In addition, I had left my glasses, journal, and money at Nadia's. My camera was safe under my sweater beneath the coat. And, that big fat wallet full of money they thought they grabbed, was an empty, folded up shopping bag. How I would have loved to see the kid's face when he unzipped the "wallet" full of nothing.

I really didn't have time to ask God for help, but I felt like He directed me to bend over each of those times. It seemed to give me balance and protection, and it slung the kid off of my back. Probably, I would not have thought to do that on my own. Isn't God good? Oh, how we praised God for these miracles.

We still had to find something to do until the registration process of my passport was complete at 4:00. We decided it was safer to talk in whispers and look around us while we walked the city. We saw the Hermitage, the Russian Museum, St. Isaac's Cathedral, Puskin Palace, Nevesky Prospect—all kinds of famous places. As we walked, we crossed bridges, water ways, alleys, side streets, and snow-covered parks. We chatted and walked and walked and walked. We were frozen and stamped our feet often to warm them. It was a great time of sightseeing and visiting. Being cold was worth it.

After the traumatic attack outside the passport office, we decided for the rest of my visit it would be safer if I walked by myself to any destinations. This way, there would not be any English spoken, and I probably would look more Russian without a Russian citizen beside me. So, that's what I did for the rest of the trip. Nadia would give me directions, point out the route on my Russian written map, and send me off.

When I had been in Russia my first time, in 1993, our group went to the Russian Museum and the Hermitage. I am not a museum person. However, one painting displayed at the Russian Museum captured my heart: *The Wave* by Ivan Aivazovsky. More than anything, I wanted to see this painting again.

Nadia gave me a hand-drawn map and said it would take two hours to walk to the museum and two hours to walk back. Truthfully, I couldn't imagine going out by myself for such a long distance. Yet, I couldn't imagine myself not going.

On my first adventure walking alone, three days after we had been attacked, I headed out to the Russian Museum. After walking the first hour to Nevesky Prospect, I saw three skinheads and some gypsies at a dumpster. They smirked and followed me with their eyes, but didn't say anything. Was I scared? Oh, yes. Absolutely petrified! I called on God for His protection fast and earnestly. In addition, I quoted Psalm 91 to myself, especially verse 14: *The LORD says, "I will rescue those who love me, I will protect those who trust in my name"* (NLT). Then, with the hope that I looked like a Russian shopper, I pulled my hood over my head and walked fast and with direct purpose. They didn't bother me. *Thank you, Lord.*

Soon I saw a Kafe (coffee) shop and decided to stop in to look at my map and get some hot tea and bread. It was a good thing I did this because I would have taken a wrong turn. I could say the map looked "Greek" to me, but actually it was in Russian, and I can't read either! You have to understand, I am pitiful with directions. Everywhere I go, I usually get lost. So for me being barely able to speak or read the language, to take a two-hour walk by myself in a foreign country…well, it was extremely scary… and exciting! It was all part of the great adventure.

While on this great walking adventure, I did try to prayer walk, but I don't think my prayers got too far. I was too busy trying to read street signs and not give in to the fear that wanted to consume me. The street mugging three days earlier was still fresh in my mind. But God, precious wonderful God, walked with me and I did get to the museum.

After checking my coat with the woman in the cloakroom, I tried to explain the painting I wanted to see. It took a while, but the woman finally understood and directed me to a back room on the second floor.

There it was. *The Wave*. The magnificent painting that had captured my heart more than 10 years earlier. I stood in awe. *The Wave* is 10 feet by 16½ feet of excellence. The oil painting shows a tumultuous, raging sea with a ship struggling to stay afloat. For some reason the magnitude and detail in this painting had me spellbound. Aivazovsky has another painting at the Russian Museum, titled *The Ninth Wave*. They aren't the same, but it's also profound. After studying *The Wave* for almost an hour, I decided I'd better leave. In Russia during winter months, it starts getting dark by 4:00 P.M. There was no way I wanted to be out by myself after dark.

With my consistent lack of directional skills, I exited the museum and had no idea which way to go. Nadia had told me to take the #169 marshrutka, shuttle bus, to get home if I didn't want to walk. Remembering the dark alley and skinheads on my walk to the museum, I decided I was up for my next challenge: locating my stop and riding the shuttle home. I climbed the steps, paid my 10 rubles and sat near to the door. Nadia had written out a sentence in Russian, so I could call it out to the driver for my stop. Ha! I practiced reading it over and over on the shuttle, but the words were so long and difficult, I couldn't get them out fast enough in one breath. This was *not* going to work.

Turning to an older man who was next to me, I asked him,

"*Vwee ga·vah reetzyah pah-ang·lees·kyah?*" (Do you speak English?).

"A little," he replied.

"Would you help me listen for this address?" I asked.

"*Dah,* I help you."

Not only did he listen, he got off the stop with me and pointed me in the direction of my home. Of course, that might have been dangerous, but I did have God with me and needed to trust a human for the one moment. The directions were perfect and took me to the apartment.

Thank you, Thank you, Thank you, God. You have walked with me all day and provided for my needs and got me home safely. Amen.

That day's solo adventure was practice for the next day's walk—to Nadia's university across town. Both Nadia and her husband had to be at the school early in the morning. So, I would start out the door completely on my own. There would be no one to point me in the right direction. "Gulp!"

The long walk was worth it. That day, Nadia had invited me to attend chapel services with her. I attended, and it was incredible. We sang and sang. It reminded me of my first trip to Russia and working with Nadia during the church services. It was an overflowing of memories of sweet Christian worship together. My soul was renewed.

For much of my trip, I continued to ask God what my purpose was for being in Russia. He reminded me it was to take the curtains and other supplies. "But God, I'm not getting the opportunity to tell anyone about you," I prayed.

You're doing exactly what I need from you.

I did not realize God's other purposes for my being in Russia in 2004 until 20 years later. They were to experience the culture as a native Russian, to gain confidence with directions, and to fully trust God. Another purpose was to give me some solo travel training for parts of my upcoming second trip to China. God always knows what we need even when we don't. When we don't understand, we still can trust Him with all the details of our lives.

Nadia and me when she came to visit in Maryland

Nadia plays in the creek

Waiting on my passport

to come home   busN169
Please, step at
ploshad' Repina.

ОСТАНОВИ́ТЕ НА ПЛО́ЩАДИ
РЕПИНА
on   she
Ostanovecte na ploshadi'
       Repina

Nadia's Russian sentences for me to call out
so the shuttle bus would stop where I needed to get off

Picnic on the Ice

Russia, 2004

N ADIA'S EYES LIT UP as she said, "Barbara, today we're taking you to the Gulf of Finland for an ice picnic. It's one of our favorite places! We'll have to walk a lot, and it's about an hour ride on the marshrutka, but I know you'll love it."

Although it was the middle of March in St. Petersburg, Russia, the bitterly cold weather remained. Snow and ice coated the sidewalks, and the local waterways were frozen solid. Not the best day for a picnic, in my opinion, but I'd read that Russians enjoyed winter picnics. Now was my opportunity to experience this unusual adventure!

Sasha, Nadia's husband, dragged his worn, leather backpack from the closet. Shaking his finger in the air, he said, "You should always have a pack with you because you never know when you'll find something useful. For example, I found these blocks of wood on the street. We can use them to build our fire today." He proceeded to stuff the wood fragments into the pack, then added matches, food, and a thermos. "Perfect," he said, and nodded.

Sasha had cooked delicious meals for us all week. *Hmmm. I wonder what kind of food he'd prepare for us to eat on an ice picnic? Probably not the American fare of fried chicken and potato salad!*

"Everybody ready?" Sasha asked as he slung his backpack over his shoulder and plopped a fur hat on his bald head.

Their older teens, Masha and Sasha, the son, nodded and moved toward the door. Nadia tucked her hair under her wool beret, then glanced at my long coat. "No." She shook her head several times. "You can't wear that coat to the place we're going. It's too nice and besides it'll get dirty. It won't be convenient for you at all."

"Oh, it's okay," I shrugged. "I can wipe it off."

A loud chorus of "no's" burst forth from the four of them.

Nadia turned and reached for another coat hanging by the door. "You must wear one of ours," she said. "Here, this will be easier for our trip. You'll see."

I knew how cold it was outside and, with a heavy heart, I removed my long, warm coat and exchanged it for the short, lightweight, blue parka she handed me. Then I threw a bright yellow scarf around my neck. I looked colorful, but doubted I'd be warm.

Sasha walked to a side table and removed an oddly-shaped key from a drawer. He unlocked the metal front door. Then he unlocked the safety bars that crossed in front of the apartment door. Earlier, they had told me this was a rough neighborhood and burglaries were frequent. After we all crowded into the hallway, he relocked and secured both the door and the bars. We tromped down the three flights of stairs, opened the street door and were slapped in the face by an artic blast. I shivered and pulled the hood of the parka over my head and tied the scarf tightly around my neck, hoping to preserve some body heat.

Our group walked for about a mile to the transit stop and stood there freezing another 30 minutes before the shuttle arrived. As usual, it was already packed with weary travelers. Tapping the snow off our boots, we climbed up, and dropped our rubles into the payment slot. As the shuttle lurched forward, we snatched the overhead handles and hung on.

I remembered the first time I was in Russia, when everyone traveled in large transport buses. Now, much of the transport was on small buses, or shuttles, called marshrutkas. It was something like a 15 passenger van, only the seats were along the side walls instead of facing forward.

We laughed, chatted, and were slung around in the shuttle as it hit every pothole in the road. More than once, I crashed into a stranger beside me. Finally, we arrived at the gulf, and immediately the bus door screeched open. I climbed down the steps. "Whoa!" I stood in ankle-deep slush and ice water. I hadn't been expecting that!

As we walked single file along the frozen docks, I soon felt an arm pass through mine. "You're not quite used to our ways," Nadia said and smiled. "I will walk with you and help."

I smiled back, "*Spasiba.*"

"You're welcome."

Nadia abruptly stopped walking and gestured to the left. "Look, Barbara."

"Wow!" My eyes widened when I saw dozens of mammoth ships stuck in the frozen water.

"They'll stay there until the gulf thaws," she said.

There also was an incredible vision of an ice community. It was my first time to see such a thing. I stared in amazement. People stood on the ice in groups or sat in chairs. Some fished; others visited or drank hot beverages together. Life went on as usual, except it was all on ice.

After walking a mile or so, Sasha pointed to a slope by the road. "Here's a great spot," he shouted. "Over here, everyone." He looked over the edge and climbed down a 15-foot snow and brush-covered embankment. His son went next, then lifted his hand to help me get down the hill. I stumbled and thrashed about, but by grabbing on to dry reeds and branches I made it to the bottom. I was surprised the frozen water was less than 10 feet away.

Sasha settled the backpack into the snow. He bent over and scooped out a small area and pounded down the snow for the base of a fire pit. Then he gathered big rocks to line the pit before arranging his wood and kindling. The rest of us carved out snow to make seats along the hill and picked up rocks to use as a seat covering.

Once Sasha had a crackling fire going, he pulled out a small bowl of pork he had pre-seasoned. From his bag, he dug out five sticks. He slid a wedge of onion and two cubes of pork on the sticks and gave one to each of us. Then he took cold, baked potatoes and arranged them around the sides of the pit. He motioned for us to move closer to the fire to grill our kabobs and, hopefully, get some warmth. Ha! Getting warm did not happen!

By the time the kabobs were cooked, the potatoes were ready. Nadia grabbed two sticks to lift a potato and place it into my mitten covered hands. Oh, that potato felt so good on my frozen fingers!

Next, Sasha reached into his pack and pulled out a loaf of bread, tearing off a chunk for each of us. We didn't use plates or utensils, but that worked for me. After all, this was an adventure! Holding my food, I scooted back into my carved-out snow seat, rested the bread on my knee, and plopped the potato on top.

I blew on the kabob and took my first bite. Oh, my goodness! It was juicy, delicious and delicately seasoned by the roasted onion. The potato was slightly charred and had crunchy skin. When I bit off a chunk my taste buds exploded at the creamy, roasted texture inside.

As a special gift, Sasha again dug into his backpack and pulled out dried raisins and apricots. "Surprise!" he said. "Now for the perfect dessert." He chuckled and gave each of us a handful of the sweet treat. Finally, he passed around two mugs filled with hot tea for us to share. My frozen body was ever so grateful for the warm, amber liquid going down my throat.

We finished eating then cleaned up the campsite. Sasha loaded the backpack, hung it over his shoulder and announced, "Time to go now. It's getting late."

We stomped around a bit to get the blood flowing back into our legs. Then we grasped branches and tree roots to pull ourselves up the frosty slope. We retraced our steps along the docks to the transit stop. The shuttle wasn't crowded this time, and God blessed by giving each of us a seat for the long ride back. We were happy, wet, frozen, and tired. It had been a lengthy day and was almost dark when we arrived home. But it had been worth it.

As we slipped our boots off at the door, Nadia mentioned how cold and wet her feet were. I noticed the soles of her shoes were worn through to her socks. She said they didn't have money for new boots, so she put cardboard in them. "Most of the time it works," she laughed. "But maybe not so well today." They did what they had to do to survive. This was life; it was usual. She massaged her toes and was grateful to have extra warm socks to cover her frozen feet. I, too, was grateful for warm socks, but my boots didn't have holes.

Later that evening, I reflected that during the trip Nadia and Sasha had given me a small piece of meat or fish each day. I knew this was a luxury and a costly sacrifice because money was tight and getting food, especially meat, wasn't easy. There weren't any grocery stores nearby, only small kiosk vendors. Public transportation was crowded and unreliable. There were long walks to the transit stop and long waits for the shuttle to arrive. Everything took time and energy. And then there was the weather. Sunny days were rare.

Nothing was easy about this delightful experience. It was familiar to them and eye-opening for me. We had traveled by foot, shuttle, and walking through ice and slush for several hours to have our picnic on the ice. It was hard. And yet, this adventure will remain one of the most memorable experiences of my life.

Every good and perfect gift is from above, coming down from the Father....
James 1:17 NIV

Nadia walking to the ice picnic area

Boats frozen in the Gulf of Finland and people walking on the ice

Me standing in front of the frozen Gulf

Eating my baked potato
while Sasha and son cook the kabobs

Nadia eating her roasted potato

Sasha father and Sasha son cook the kabobs as Masha watches

Sasha holding a kabob

Sasha father eating a potato while Sasha son pours a cup of hot tea

Russian Potato Salad

Ingredients

    8 medium potatoes, peeled
    ½ cucumber peeled, seeded, and finely chopped
    1 green pepper, diced
    1 medium onion, chopped
    1½ cups sour cream
    2 carrots, peeled and finely chopped
    salt and pepper to taste

    Optional: Chopped tomatoes also may be added, if desired.

Instructions

1) Peel and boil potatoes; they should be tender but slightly firm.
2) Drain potatoes well.
3) Cool potatoes and cut into large cubes.
4) Peel and chop carrots into small cubes.
5) Place chopped potatoes in a large bowl. Add all chopped vegetables. Mix gently.
6) Add salt and pepper to taste.
7) Stir in sour cream.
8) Refrigerate for at least 1 hour before serving.

Measurements do not have to be exact in this salad. The key is to use sour cream, not mayonnaise!

Serves 8-10

NOTE: The country was too poor when I visited Russia, so I did not have this favorite dish. However, a Russian gave this recipe to me.

Updates on Moldovan Friends

2024

MY LAST TRIP TO MOLDOVA made an indelible impact on me because these people were recovering from a severe drought during which both people and crops had perished. I won't ever be the same. My prayer is: *God, how can I help? How can I make a difference? In Moldova? In America? In Jesus' name. Amen.*

In September 2023, James and I were blessed to visit with Igor in North Carolina while he was in the States. We also met his wife, Christina, and their youngest son, Bogden. After over 25 years of separation, what a joyous reunion it was!

I no longer hear from Mashie or Oxana, but I do have an update on Rasita, Zhanna, and Igor.

Rasita is in her 80s. She has difficulty seeing. However, she continues to serve those in her community as much as she is physically able.

Zhanna is married with two older children and is retired from her medical job as an army physician.

Igor is married and has three sons and a daughter. As a pastor, he ministers to youth and college students. He has been arrested twice for sharing the Gospel message where he lives in Tiraspol, in the Transnistria area. Transnistria, while not "officially" communist, is still communist controlled and governed.

Since the ongoing war between Ukraine and Russia, Igor and his church are involved in distributing food, clothing, and other supplies to the Ukrainian refugees who have fled across the border to Transnistria. He and his wife, Christina, have daily opportunities to share the Gospel with the homeless survivors of the war through Bible studies, children's camps, arts and crafts, feeding stations, church services, and other needs that arise.

In addition to the refugee work, Igor's congregation, Church Without Walls, uses holidays such as Easter and Christmas to prepare tea and gifts for the community in order to reach people for Christ.

Igor's steadfast work reminds me of Paul's words of encouragement:

Therefore, my dear brothers and sisters, stand firm, let nothing move you. Always give yourselves fully to the work of the Lord, because you know that your labor in the Lord is not in vain.

1 Corinthians 15:58 NIV

STORIES JUST FOR FUN

The Uninvited Guest

Texas, 1992

I FELT ITS PRESENCE before I saw it. Glancing around the living room, I saw nothing was out of place. I scanned the room again and found it staring at me. My heart pounded as I slammed my book shut and quickly pulled my feet off the floor. A blood-curdling scream followed my action, "Jaaames! Tarantula!"

My poor husband roused from a deep sleep and jumped from his recliner. He wobbled back and forth as his eyes fluttered trying to focus. He mumbled out a slurred, "Huh? What? What's wrong?"

"Tarantula! Get it! Get it!" My arms flailed over my head.

There sat this huge, black creature next to an orange pillow on the sofa. We lived in Texas where tarantulas were common during the hot summers, but this was my first time to encounter such a beast. For it to invade my house and make itself at home…well, it just wasn't right. Something had to be done and I bequeathed the task to my still-traumatized husband.

What do you do with a huge, hairy spider bigger than your

hand? You certainly can't squish it.

"James, you've got to get rid of it. Hurry!" My voice escalated another octave.

"How?" He began to wake up, and walked over to the door.

"What are you doing?"

"I'm going to let it out the door."

"No! You can't do that. He may come back. You've got to catch it," I insisted.

"I'll see if I can find something from the kitchen to use." He rubbed his eyes, not enjoying his assignment one bit. "You keep an eye on 'Hairy T' while I look around."

I heard cabinet doors opening, drawers banging shut, and other rattles I couldn't recognize. About 10 minutes later, he returned to the living room grinning and bearing a tarantula catcher. He'd found a long broom handle and taped one of my wide plastic bowls around the side of it. It resembled a toilet plunger, only without the suction part.

I glimpsed back to the sofa. I guess Hairy T had seen the tarantula catcher, too.

"Oh, no! He's gone! Hurry, start searching."

James dashed to the sofa and moved the orange pillow. He lifted the other orange pillow. No Hairy T. I tucked my feet further into the seat of my chair while James lifted up the sofa and tilted it against the wall.

"There he is! He's on the floor. Get him, quick," I said pointing to the corner next to the edge of the sofa.

Hairy T, or "H T" for short, calmly sat there waiting and watching. My mind surged into overdrive. It looked to me like he'd grown six inches.

James wasn't too thrilled to be the one to conquer H T's invasion; but since he was the man of the house, I deemed it a fitting task for him. Biting his lip, with the tarantula catcher ready for battle, James got into *en garde* position. I could see he was nervous.

James took a deep breath and plunged toward the beast. "Got him!" H T was now under the cover of my plastic bowl and not too happy. He thumped his legs under the clear plastic and scratched the sides of the bowl.

"Hold tight, Sweetie. Don't let him escape." I untangled my legs from the chair. "Let me see if I can find something to slide under the bowl."

James continued to press the tarantula catcher onto the floor, and, with profuse sweating and trembling, I slid a cookie sheet under the bowl. H T hopped around and banged against the bowl as he was scooted onto the tin sheet.

What in the world were we going to do with him now? I'd caught a snake once by covering it with a trashcan and then scooting a cookie sheet under it. Afterward, I'd carried it out to a field and flung all three as far as I could. Maybe that would work again.

"I've got an idea. James, you take all this stuff and *you* get rid of H T."

He looked at me like I was crazy. The team work had just ended and now he had total possession of the hairy beast.

It was midnight. We'd been working on our capture since 10:45. In my mind, H T now was almost as big as a Thanksgiving turkey. I unlocked the front door and the three of us went out onto the sidewalk.

"James, go stand in the middle of the street and walk straight down the road for about two blocks. I'll stand here and watch you. Oh, I think you should also shake the bowl up and down while you're walking, so H T will get dizzy. When you get two blocks away, open the tarantula catcher away from you and fling out the beast. Then turn around and run back as fast as you can. Okay?"

"Okay," James said. "I think that'll work."

There's nothing like standing in the middle of the road at midnight watching your husband walk away into the dark abyss while carrying a 10-pound tarantula. He vanished. I was scared for him. Suppose the tarantula got loose and bit him? I was scared for me. Suppose someone came up behind me and tried to grab me?

After too much quiet, I heard the echo of running feet, but I couldn't see where they were coming from. Was it James, or some questionable character in my questionable neighborhood? With relief, I saw my husband racing up the street. He had gone several blocks past the designated two blocks to make sure H T didn't find his way back. He panted hard and was soaking wet when he arrived. I ushered both of us into the house and quickly locked the door behind us. We did a thorough search of the house, hoping H T hadn't brought other uninvited guests with him.

We calmed down a little and headed off to bed. Neither of us slept well. The ceiling fan with the circling brown paddles seemed like thrashing tarantula legs above our heads all night. The next morning we compared stories. Both of us had dreams of tarantulas invading our home.

About a week later, I got home from work around 6 P.M. Depositing a bag of groceries by the front door, I went back to the car for another bag. I turned around, and what did I see? No, it wasn't Hairy T. Most likely it was Mrs. Hairy T! I dropped the bag. Before I could stop myself, I screamed out another blood-curdling "Jaames! Tarantula!"

In less than a minute, the front door flung open and my knight in shining armor rushed out carrying a cookie sheet and the plastic tarantella catcher. I stood almost paralyzed as my knight scooped up Mrs. Hairy T. "I'll be back in a minute," he winked. "I need to walk a few blocks down the street...."

No Child Was Eaten

Maryland

THE FORSYTHIA BUSHES WERE BURSTING with curly, yellow blossoms. It was now time to sweep out the house and feed the alligators.

Mrs. Cathy had the most Forsythia bushes in our Baltimore neighborhood. Three to be exact. These giant wonders were taller than the railing on her four-step porch. From my five-year-old perspective, they were the prettiest flowers in the whole wide world, and I stretched my little arms out to prove it.

I lived in a neighborhood with a long grassy plot in the middle of a courtyard surrounded by 20 row houses. There were 10 houses on one side and 10 on the other side. This huge patch of grass served as a kickball field, tug-of-war boundary, garden for tea parties with dollies, and anything else 20 children could imagine.

Not only did we kids have this terrific grassy play area, we also had a sidewalk that circled it. It wasn't uncommon to see a line of tricycles racing around the corners of the courtyard, with handlebar streamers blowing in the wind, or perhaps it was the red wagon brigade toting teddy bears for an impromptu parade.

Our courtyard was a total playground, but without any seesaws, swings, or slides.

Most of the kids living there were four and five years old. I was the tallest, except for Mrs. Jane's Billy. He was two inches taller than me. Somehow that made both of us leaders. And most of the time, we chose what everyone played next.

Behind Mrs. Cathy's Forsythias was the perfect playhouse. There was about a three-foot by eight-foot space between the bushes and the wall of her house. A slight gap between the bushes became the front door. As soon as someone pushed through them, the bushes whooshed back together and the door was closed.

The space allowed us kids to set up housekeeping. The basement window was a foot from the ground, so the ledge around it became the oven for cooking our mud pies. The top step became the kitchen cabinet and held our red and blue metal teacups and saucers. It also housed our green plastic berry baskets, cut off milk cartons, and the various sizes of twigs that we used as silverware. The next step held our Play-Doh meat, green beans, and rock and stone biscuits. It was more than adequate for our appetites.

To go behind the yellow bushes was like entering a fairyland. Sometimes our spot was a bakery. Kids would ring the metal bell on their trikes, and the worker for the day would give curbside service. Other days a busy little housekeeper would sweep and sweep, trying to get her dirt floor clean.

Some days we would peek into the basement window and watch Mrs. Cathy hang her wet clothes on the sagging lines strung between the stairs and the hook on the wall.

But the best thing of all about the bushes was that they

provided us food to "feed the alligators." All of us—preschoolers and kindergarteners alike—would gather by the Forsythias and grab two big fistfuls of blossoms. Wide-eyed and with legs shaking, we gathered around the sides of the grassy oval courtyard. It was time. Billy would tell us to throw our food fast and far and then run as hard as we could. We all knew alligators loved to snack on children's arms and legs. (Alligators don't eat heads, though, because the hair gets stuck in their teeth and they don't have toothbrushes.)

When Billy gave us the signal—a wave of his arm—screams from 20 children penetrated the air as hundreds of blossoms flew into the grassy pit. "Alligators" swished and flailed to chomp on the delectable morsels.

No child was eaten.

Only when all the alligators were fed and sleepy did all of us gather under the shade tree on the corner. We compared stories of who saw the biggest alligator, who had the most flowers to throw, and who was the most scared.

The area including the courtyard and behind the Forsythias was our magic kingdom. It was here that we played cowboys and Indians, Mother-May-I, Red Light Green Light, tag, and more. It was our safe place, except, of course, when we fed the alligators.

It was a kid's world, a kind of heaven on earth. It only became a bad dream when the moms came out of the houses and called their cherished young uns in for lunch, a nap, or worst of all…a bath!

Pete Bites the Dust

Tennessee, 2016

I HEARD THE THUMP and saw the color of rust fly in front of the car and smack the ground.

"Oh no! That was a robin!"

The bird lay still. I got to my feet to peer through the blinds. Was it hurt or worse, dead?

I named it Pete.

Jeans and a shirt were close, so I pulled them over my pj's. Next I found a thin tray that would serve as a scoop to bring Pete back to the house.

By now tears ran down my face.

"Poor bird, I hope he's not in pain."

With tray in hand, I threw open the door and ran to the road. It didn't look like Pete had been hit again, but he also didn't move or chirp.

"He's dead!" More tears.

I bent down to slide Pete onto my tray. "Where's the rest of his body?"

Then I knew the truth.

It wasn't a robin on the road. It was a clump of red Tennessee clay that had fallen from under the car.

"Red clay! Had I truly wept over a clump of red clay?"

My grief was raw. The pain was real. Now I felt silly and hoped no one saw me.

Pete the clump, got a swift kick and flew to the other side of the road.

Back in the house, I wiped my eyes, blew my nose, and made a cup of tea. I got a pen and paper, sat at my desk, and began to write Pete's obit.

Now That's a Nice-a Meatball

Maryland, 1984

Mmmm, I could smell the aroma of the garlic and other Italian spices even before I opened the front door. It smelled heavenly. Uncle Vince was coming to dinner tonight and Mama had worried about it all day.

As the only non-Italian in the family, Mama wanted to impress Uncle Vince—who was the "Italian of Italians" in the D'Antoni clan. While he had eaten with us several times before, it was never for an Italian dinner. Mama had simmered homemade spaghetti sauce all day and made extra big meatballs just like my Italian Grandma did.

About an hour before Uncle Vince arrived, Mama grabbed the bag of meatballs she had cooked and frozen two days before. She carefully ladled the meatballs into the bubbling pot of sauce.

The salad was made and covered with a damp towel to keep it crisp, the table set, the garlic bread ready to pop into the oven, and the pot of water for the spaghetti almost at a boil. Perfect!

Uncle Vince arrived about 20 minutes early. No problem. We did the Italian kissing-on-the-cheek thing. Then he and

Daddy sat in the living room to "shoot the breeze" while Mama and I dished up the food.

"Come on in guys. Food's about to be served." Mama smiled confidently.

I passed Uncle Vince the bowl piled with spaghetti. He scooped up a big portion. Then Daddy handed him the platter of meatballs. When he saw the size of them, his eyes widened and he licked his lips. He wiggled his eyebrows up and down and then helped himself to three meatballs, while Mama held her breath.

Chewing on a piece of crusty garlic bread, he twirled spaghetti around his fork and put it in his mouth. He gave a nod of approval. "Great sauce, Nellie." Mama breathed and burst into a big smile.

Then he speared a meatball and took a huge bite. He paused and blinked, "Interesting texture and spices in these meatballs, Hon. Different, but they're good." Mama relaxed. In fact, the meatballs were so good, Uncle Vince had two more. Mama beamed with joy. She knew she had passed the test.

The next morning while I made coffee, Mama opened the freezer door to remove a roast for dinner. She gasped, threw her hand over her mouth and stood pointing at something.

"Mama, what's wrong?" I touched her shoulder.

She kept pointing. When she finally spoke, she said, "Oh, Barb, *that's* the bag of meatballs."

I just laughed at her. "Mom, we ate them last night for dinner!"

She shook her head in disbelief and said, "*No, we didn't.* A couple of days ago, I made a dozen bran muffins, because

I know how much you like them. I even put in raisins and extra cinnamon." She shut the freezer door and leaned her head against it.

"I can't believe it. I must have grabbed the wrong bag and put the bran muffins in the spaghetti sauce!"

"What are you going to do?" I asked. "Are you going to tell Daddy and Uncle Vince?"

"Nothing. I'm going to do absolutely nothing," she looked up and grinned. "And don't you tell either! But I'll say this, everyone's going to have healthier systems today…and Uncle Vince will be the healthiest of all!"

Bran Muffins

Ingredients

    1 cup all-purpose flour

    ¼ cup honey

    1½ cup wheat bran

    ¼ cup molasses

    1 teaspoon baking soda

    1 cup milk

    ¼ teaspoon salt

    1 egg

    2 tablespoons oil

    ¾ cup raisins

    Optional: Ground cinnamon and ground cloves to taste

                  Almond or vanilla extract to taste

Instructions

1. Preheat oven to 400°.
2. Mix together all ingredients.
3. Fill lightly greased muffin pan ¾ full.
4. Bake for 20 minutes.

Makes 12 muffins.

Good plain, with butter, marmalade, or peanut butter.

Freezes well.

NOTE: Can also be made with oat bran, instead of wheat bran.

CONCLUSION

Suppose I Hadn't Listened

Texas, 1986

***T**HE MAN SITTING IN THE CAR under that tree on the right is going to follow you.*

"Whoa! Where did that come from?" I felt like it might be a prompt from God because He had warned me in the past of upcoming danger. My first response to the prompt was, "Nah. This is crazy," but I did pay attention to the car parked under the tree.

It was 8:30 p.m. and I was on my way home from work. I waited for traffic to pass so I could make the left turn that headed to my apartment in Fort Worth, Texas.

I passed the car under the tree and turned on my blinker for the right turn into my complex. The car pulled out behind me and turned right also.

My apartment was immediately to the right, but I bypassed it and kept driving. The car continued to follow me. This was a huge complex, with maybe 400 apartments and lots of twists and turns. I drove through most of the sections trying to see if the car would follow. It did. Finally, I came to a dead end with a curb. The man thought he had cornered me, so he got out of his car and ran toward me. Backing up a few yards, I put the car into drive and floored it, jumping the curb into another parking lot. The man hurried back to his car and he did the same.

Uh, oh. This isn't good! I no longer drove slowly or carefully. My goal was to get out of there fast! This had never happened to me before. My heart raced and my breath came out in puffs as I grasped the steering wheel and tried not to wreck the car. The fear I experienced was almost overwhelming.

Speeding along the road, I left the complex, turned left past the tree and swerved back to the road where God had given me the prompt. The car behind me screeched onto the main road as well. I glanced into my rearview mirror and saw not one man, but two! Apparently the second man had been crouched down to remain hidden. The fast and reckless driving, however, had forced him upright.

As I turned left again, I screamed, "God, what do I do? What do I do?"

Very clearly, I heard, *Use the horn.* I pressed the horn and held my hand on it. Not far ahead, I saw a stop sign.

"God, stop sign ahead. Now what?"

Go through it.

"Okay." With my hand continuing to sound the horn, I ran the stop sign. The car following me did also. "Help me, God! I'm scared."

The men's dorm is up ahead, turn right into the parking lot.

"Okay, okay, I will." At this point the car following me was practically on my bumper. Still blowing the horn, I waited until I was almost past the second entrance and jerked the wheel to the right, swerving into the parking lot. This was so sudden the car behind me didn't have time to make the turn, so it passed me.

Of course, all the noise from my horn and the loud screech of my tires in the street brought a lot of men running to my car. By now I was crying and hysterical. Several men surrounded my car and asked if I was okay. I explained about the car following me. They promised to stay with me until I felt safe enough to return home.

There will never be enough gratitude in my heart to God for all He did for me that night. He warned me, then directed my steps by giving me answers when I screamed out in terror. He protected me from the men in the other car, and He watched over me on the road and through the stop sign. Finally, He gave me a group of men from the seminary to surround my car. When God first gave me that prompt, I thought it was a bit far-fetched, and I almost ignored it. Suppose, just suppose, I hadn't listened….

Thank you, Lord, for watching over me even when I wanted to doubt You.

Over the years, people have ridiculed me for my faith in God. I've heard more times than once, "What do you mean, God told you? Who are you that God speaks to you?" Quite frankly, I am His child and God talks to His children. Why wouldn't He talk to me, or you? It is not unusual for God to speak to us. It's His desire to have a relationship with each of us.

The Bible states that, even though God is holy, He loves sinful people so much He allowed Jesus, His only Son, to die for each of us, so that all who believe in Jesus would have eternal life with Him (John 3:16 paraphrased).

My young life had a lot of pain and sorrow in it. When I invited Jesus into my life at age 11½, I took seriously the promise that God wants a relationship with me. God was and is my refuge, my safe place. This promise is for everyone. I have never regretted this decision.

Dozens of times the Bible tells us that God will never leave or abandon us. I have found it to be the truth. In the times that I chose to follow my own selfish, sinful desires, God walked through the dirt with me. He kept His promise and never abandoned me. I remember telling Him many times, "God, you don't belong here. You are too holy to be in this sinful environment." While I'm sure my actions grieved His heart, He walked the road with me anyway. He has been faithful.

God always answers my prayers, but I don't always like the answers. His answers can be no, yes, not now, or I will walk through this pain with you. I trust Him enough to know whatever He decides for my life is the best for me.

Before and during all of the trips I've written about, I listened to God's directions. Not always happily, and sometimes "kicking and screaming."

Suppose I hadn't listened?

I would have missed out on some of the richest and most precious experiences of my life. So now, I give Him all the praise and honor He deserves.

Glory to God in the Highest!

Acknowledgments

T**his book would not be possible** without the help of my beloved husband, James. He did all the typing for me. In addition, he read aloud all the stories so I could hear them. Thank you JBD. I love you.

Lisa and Greg Williams—Oh, my, where to start? You have done so much for us in the last four years. Thank you for all your encouragement and support throughout this entire process.

Thank you Dr. Vicki Barker for spending countless hours enthusiastically encouraging me, reading, and editing my stories. Bless you, friend.

Dr. Ellen Millsaps, my freshman English professor (1979). Thank you for believing in me and encouraging me to write. That was the beginning.

A very special thank you to my new friend, Glenn Fuqua, who I met at a writers conference earlier in 2024. Glenn took the fabulous photo of the plane wing and was gracious enough to allow me to use it for this book.

Thank you to my editor and publisher, Terri Kalfas, at Grace Publishing. I am grateful for her similar vision and suggestions of ministry for the book. She made this book possible.

Thank you to all my friends who continued to say, "We love your stories; you have to write a book." Here it is, friends. I hope you enjoy it. I would list your names, but I know I would forget someone, and that would break my heart. So consider yourself loved, appreciated, and hugged.

Finally, I thank my beloved Lord and Savior, Jesus Christ. To You I give all the glory, honor and praise You deserve.

Scriptures Meaningful to Me

Philippians 4:8 NLT

> *And now, dear brothers and sisters, let me say one more thing as I close this letter.*
>
> *Fix your thoughts on what is true and honorable and right.*
>
> *Think about things that are pure and lovely and admirable.*
>
> *Think about things that are excellent and worthy of praise.*

1 Corinthians 15:58 NIV

> *Therefore my dear brothers and sisters, stand firm. Let nothing move you. Always give yourselves fully to the work of the Lord, because you know that your labor in the Lord is not in vain.*

Philippians 1:21 NIV
> *For to me, to live is Christ, and to die is gain.*

About the Author

Author Barbara D'Antoni Diggs shares heart-touching God moments from her national and international experiences by writing creative non-fiction.

One of her stories was selected to be included in *Chicken Soup for the Soul: Laughter's Always the Best Medicine*.

For five years, Barbara wrote a column for her church newsletter. Her mission articles have appeared in *Contempo* and *Royal Service* magazines. She is published in two anthologies, and has guest blogged for *We, a Great Parade*.

As a retired ESL instructor, Barbara continues to enjoy visiting with people from other countries and trying their ethnic foods. Learning words in other languages will definitely bring a light to her eyes. She speaks some, but not enough, Russian, Japanese, Chinese, French, Spanish and American Sign Language.

She and her husband, James, make their home in east Tennessee.

www.ingramcontent.com/pod-product-compliance
Lightning Source LLC
Chambersburg PA
CBHW040302170426
43194CB00021B/2865